P9-EDF-342

SURPLUS
DUPLICATE

A GUIDE TO
COMMUNIST JARGON

Also by
R. N. CAREW HUNT
THE THEORY AND PRACTICE OF COMMUNISM
MARXISM, PAST AND PRESENT

12476

R. N. CAREW HUNT

A GUIDE TO
COMMUNIST JARGON

NEW YORK

THE MACMILLAN COMPANY

1957

82758

HX17
H91

© R. N. Carew Hunt 1957

All rights reserved—no part of this book may be reproduced in any
form without permission in writing from the publisher, except by a
reviewer who wishes to quote brief passages in connection with a
review written for inclusion in magazine or newspaper.

First Printing

Printed in the United States of America

Library of Congress catalog card number: 57-11711

PROPERTY OF UNITED STATES

CONTENTS

Introduction (*page* vii)

INTRODUCTION

MARXISM–LENINISM, the official creed of Communism, has given rise to a number of political or semi-political concepts which Communists use in explaining or defending their position. The purpose of this book is to enquire into the meaning of the more important of these, and to show how they are related to one another. It should be noted that the Russian Communist Party (and in consequence other Communist Parties also) has always attached great importance to the principles for which it stands, and to the duty of every party member to master them as far as he is able, in which it follows Lenin, who had declared early in his career that "without a revolutionary theory there can be no revolutionary movement". Indeed, Communism would not be what it is today if a great many people did not hold its creed to be altogether superior to that of any other political party, and the often-raised and rather unintelligent question as to how far the Russian or other communist leaders believe in it has little relevance. In any case, the word "believe" has many shades of meaning.

It is as well to make this point clear from the outset, because anyone who deals with the type of theoretical concept which will be examined in these pages exposes himself, and not least in this country, to the charge that he is wasting his time. Thus it is argued that the ordinary Soviet citizen, and Communists generally, do not really take these concepts seriously. Indeed, for some time past visitors to the Soviet Union who have had an opportunity of establishing contact with Russians of all classes have recorded that the attitude adopted towards the official ideology, particularly by the younger generation, is commonly one of indifference and even of ridicule. Yet this need not surprise us. In the years immediately following the October Revolution the ideas which had inspired it had a potency which they cannot be expected to possess today. In no society in which a regime has been long established is it to be expected that the majority will be interested in the exposition and discussion of political abstractions, especially if these are continually thrust upon them from above. Soviet citizens have had to endure years of intensive theoretical indoctrination, conducted through every known medium of propaganda, and it is perfectly intelligible that they should have become weary of it, the more so as those who possess any critical sense will have found it difficult to account for its constant shifts. In the autumn of 1956 a new scheme of ideological training was issued, of which particulars were published in *Kommunist* of October, and a ruling was given as to which of Stalin's writings were still to be regarded as canonical. This was indeed called for, since such uncertainty had prevailed in the preceding summer that the Party schools had found it necessary to suspend their examinations in Marxist–Leninist theory, while in the High Schools and Universities, which could not do this, as the subject formed part of the regular curriculum, candidates were instructed to base their answers as far as possible on the decisions of the Twentieth Congress. Yet it does not follow from the above that the majority of Russians do not "believe" in their "idea", or that they are prepared to change it for another. And in any event, the concepts which collectively make up the official ideology deserve attention as representing what the leaders have every reason for wishing the public to believe.

For this ideology serves the double purpose of seeking to provide a rational basis for the Soviet form of society and system of government, and a justification for their control by the Communist Party. As the revolution led to consequences very different from those which its authors had anticipated, the ideology that emerged from it was inevitably a distorted one, and came increasingly to involve that process which George Orwell has described as "double think". There is, for example, nothing "democratic" about "proletarian democracy" except the use of the term "democracy", which has been retained for obvious reasons. It is only one of a number of concepts which have been excogitated in order to defend the Soviet regime and uphold the claims of the Party. But this, in itself, does not affect the question as to whether Communists may not accept such concepts, seeing that at no period has it proved difficult to persuade large numbers of persons to adopt positions to which neither common sense nor an appeal to readily ascertainable facts lends support.

At first sight it may seem strange that the Communists, who profess to be materialists, should attach a far greater significance to ideas than their opponents whom they style idealists. Yet it is intelligible enough. The younger a movement the more conscious will it be of its theoretical basis, which an older movement will tend to take for granted. Further, the Left-Wing is always more given to theorizing than the Right. To the Conservative, the stratified form which society assumes if it is left to itself, though doubtless subject to abuses which require to be rectified, is upon the whole salutary and desirable as conforming to a natural order of things under which the more industrious and intelligent tend to rise above their fellows. His instinct bids him interfere with this process as little as possible. On the other hand, the Socialist regards such a society as fundamentally inequitable, and holds that it is for the State to remodel it in accordance with the principles of "social justice". As to what these principles are, and how best the State can give effect to them, there is naturally a diversity of opinion, and thus a corresponding proliferation of political, social and economic theories.

The form of totalitarianism that we call Communism represents this left-wing attitude of mind extended to its ultimate limit. For, as J. L. Talmon points out, totalitarianism recognizes only one plane of action, the political, and widens the scope of politics to embrace the whole of human existence, so that everything men think or do becomes charged with social significance, and has therefore to be brought under regulation and control. Politics thus becomes the art of applying this philosophy to the organization of society, and its final purpose will only be achieved when everything has been subjected to it.[1]

It is this that gives Communism its peculiarly fanatical character. It has often been pointed out that it is a secular religion (or we may prefer to call it a faith), so that it has its heaven and hell, its elect and damned, its sacred books and those alone competent to interpret them. The authors of the October Revolution set out to abolish Capitalism and transfer the means of production to the workers, who, it was assumed, would be competent to administer them efficiently. The first of these objectives was attained easily enough, but the second was to prove far more difficult, as the economy of the country virtually collapsed and, contrary to Lenin's expectations, the proletariat of the West refused to rise and come to its assistance. Gradually it became apparent that the transition from Capitalism to Socialism—to say nothing of the further passage into the "higher stage" of Communism—would be an extremely arduous task, and one which would incidentally call for far-reaching changes in human nature. Yet the building of a new society is the supreme goal of Communism, and has an absolute value, so that any measure is justified which promotes its attainment.

[1] *The Origins of Totalitarian Democracy*, (1952), p. 3.

As the instrument for building this society is the Communist Party, anyone who opposes its policy is *eo ipso* obstructing the realization of the society itself. Such persons must therefore be ruthlessly eliminated, and the false ideas which inspire their opposition be systematically exposed. For the guardians of the communist faith are fully alive to the existence of heresies that pervert it, and have discovered a large number of them. The reader of communist propaganda will therefore find himself confronted with numerous terms which may be strange to him, and with others the meaning of which is not what he has hitherto supposed. Many of them are injurious epithets hurled at the non-communist world, or at Communist Parties and at their leaders who are held to be influenced by its ideology. Their meaning is seldom defined at the time, while their nature is such that one will often do as well as another, just as if we turn to what we may call the communist vocabulary of zoological vituperation, it does not much matter whether an opponent is called a jackal or a hyena. The fact that some of the terms we shall be considering are so related that they deal with the same issue from a slightly different angle has thus made it impossible, in discussing them, to avoid a certain amount of repetition.

A few of these terms are to be found in the writings of Marx and Engels, but most of them were coined by Lenin, from whom they were taken over by Stalin. Some have their origin in the peculiar situation in Russia at the time when Lenin was first becoming active on the political stage, and which led him to demand such a party as would inevitably tend to display shortcomings of a particular type. Others may be traced to his doctrine of the transition of Capitalism from the industrial into the imperialist phase, which he held to have created a "revolutionary situation" calling for the adoption of new tactics which were equally liable to be misused. Others, again, date from his attack on the Second International during and immediately after the First World War. But whatever their source, they have led to the emergence of a new political vocabulary. Imperialism, for example, has become so closely associated with its historical progenitor, Capitalism, that the "capitalists" of Marx and Engels have become the "imperialists" of contemporary communist propaganda.

If, however, these terms are to be understood, they must be related to certain fundamental propositions to which the world-revolutionary movement, under the aegis of Moscow, has given rise. Of these, the more important are the following:

(1) Communism is essentially a revolutionary movement which holds that the entire structure of society must be changed, and denies that this can be achieved by peaceful means, or at least that this is possible in any country in which the bourgeoisie opposes it.

(2) The October Revolution made it possible, for the first time in history, to set up a multi-national socialist State. This is the prototype of the future socialist World-State, which will be based upon the same principles.

(3) As a result of the revolution, the world has become divided into two hostile camps—the socialist and the imperialist. The former has always been "under the leadership of the Soviet Union", whereas the leadership of the latter has been assigned to whichever country the Soviet Government has regarded as its principal enemy at the time. In the 'twenties it was ascribed to Britain, and after the rise of Hitler to Nazi Germany. In his Cominform speech of September 1947 Zhdanov declared that it was exercised by "Anglo-American imperialism", for which, in 1948, Stalin substituted "American imperialism and its satellites", the implication being that the war had so seriously weakened Britain that the country had now become an American dependency.

(4) It is expedient for tactical reasons to declare that the "peaceful coexistence" of the two camps is possible, and at times the internal situation of the Soviet Union makes it especially desirable to emphasize this. The conditions under which it is possible are not, however, clearly defined, nor would this be easy, seeing that dialectical and historical materialism not only assume a conflict between the two, but also that it must end with the victory of Socialism, as this is "in the line of history". This belief in the inevitability of Socialism rests upon the Marxist–Leninist analysis according to which the progress of society depends on the evolution of the productive forces, which are hampered under Capitalism, and can be fully developed only under a socialist economy.

(5) It is the task of Communist Parties to hasten forward the victory of Socialism. But this will only be achieved if these parties accept the leadership of the Soviet Union, which alone combines the necessary revolutionary experience and material resources. Any refusal to accept it is an indication of "bourgeois nationalism" as opposed to that "proletarian internationalism" upon which the relations between socialist countries are allegedly based. Here, until recently, Tito was held up as the chief offender, as he was represented as claiming that it was possible to build "Socialism in one country" without the aid of the Soviet Union and of the world proletariat.

(6) The communist movement will inevitably encounter the hostility of the non-communist world, and this will be especially directed against the Soviet Union as its citadel. That capitalists should adopt this attitude is only to be expected, as they will naturally not wish to be deprived of the privileged position which enables them to oppress their own workers and those of the countries they exploit. The real enemies of the working class are, however, the Social Democratic (or Socialist) Parties, and particularly their right-wing leaders, but

for whose support the capitalists would be unable to retain power. This animosity is in part due to the fact that these parties are rivals with the Communists for the leadership of the masses, and in part to the "all-or-nothing" nature of communist thinking, which leads to the rejection as "opportunism" of whatever stops short of the absolute goal of revolution.

(7) The Soviet Union stands for peace, and the imperialists for war, in which they are once again supported by their socialist "lackeys". This was the burden of the much-advertised "peace campaign", the biggest propaganda drive ever undertaken. It was an extremely clever move, as it not only provided cover for the aggressive policy simultaneously adopted by the Cominform, but also contrived to associate in the confused thinking of large sections of the public the desire to preserve peace and their various political, social and economic grievances.

(8) One of the most formidable weapons of the imperialist camp is the ideological one. "Bourgeois ideology", from which, for polemical purposes, that of Social Democracy is represented as indistinguishable, is forever seeking to corrupt the citizens of the Soviet Union and its satellites, and any capitulation to it is a betrayal of the proletarian cause. Thus it must be combated by "revolutionary vigilance", and by intensifying ideological training, the importance of which is everlastingly stressed. This training, or indoctrination, is designed to explain the principles upon which the communist system rests, and to demonstrate their superiority by contrasting the progress made in the Soviet Union and the well-being of its citizens with the decadence of the West and the insecurity of its workers. It is empirical inasmuch as the authorities continually insist that it must be related to practical issues, so that not much attention is paid, at least on the lower levels, to purely theoretical questions, though these are studied exhaustively in the

higher centres of communist learning, and articles upon them constantly appear.

That many of the terms discussed were first given currency in the Soviet Union does not render it impermissible to refer to them as "communist", seeing that all Communist Parties accept them and make use of them in their press and propaganda. The basis of selection has been their employment since the late war in the Russian press and other publications and in the *Cominform Journal*. For their definition, the principal sources used have been, (a) The 1952 edition of the *Large Soviet Encyclopædia*, and articles in it passed for publication at later dates, (b) *The Political Dictionary* (1940), re-issued in 1956, edited by G. F. Aleksandrov, V. Galyanov and N. Rubenshtein, (c) *The Short Philosophical Dictionary* (1939), re-issued in 1941, 1951–52, and 1954, edited by M. Rozenthal and P. Yudin, (d) S. E. Ozhegov's *Dictionary of the Russian Language* (1952), (e) D. N. Ushakov's *Dictionary of the Russian Language* (1935 and 1952), and (f) E. V. Lyekhin's *Dictionary of Foreign Words* (1949). Articles in the more important Soviet theoretical periodicals, e.g., *Problems of Philosophy* and *Kommunist*, have also been consulted. The *Cominform Journal* is a secondary source only, as its leaders and articles faithfully repeated whatever was the official doctrine as set out, for example, in *The Short Philosophical Dictionary*, an invaluable work which it is probable that every communist editor keeps upon his table.

It has been necessary to make frequent citations from the works of Lenin and Stalin, and occasionally from those of Marx and Engels, as these form the canon of the communist scriptures. As, however, this book is intended for the general reader, footnotes giving references to the passages quoted have not been added, but the titles of the particular writings in which they appear have been given.

In conclusion, some critics will doubtless argue that although the account of communist ideology given in these pages may represent fairly enough what the position was at the time of Stalin's death, it has ceased to be applicable to the post-Stalinist period. Certainly there has been a change, and it is perhaps most observable in connection with the application of "socialist realism", the principle to which literature, music and the arts are required to conform, and which has exhibited "party-mindedness" in its most fanatical form. Novelists, for example, are no longer obliged to accept the fiction that the worker is inspired solely by his desire to assist the Soviet Union, and it is now permissible to admit the existence of other and more natural motives, such as the desire to earn more money or to get on in the world. Today books are appearing which, in their criticism of Soviet conditions, go far beyond that of Zoshchenko, whose two best-known works, *Before the Sunrise* and *The Adventure of an Ape*, were condemned in 1947. Yet what is significant is that Zoshchenko has not been rehabilitated. The judgment against him stands, and may still be invoked, seeing that the Zhdanovite decrees on literature, though now admitted to contain certain "factual inaccuracies and false generalizations", have never been officially repudiated, and were upheld in *Kommunist* as recently as October 1956. Similarly, it has been pointed out officially, in connection with the disorders in Poland, that the doctrine of "separate paths to Socialism" does not invalidate the "leading role" of the Russian Communist Party, which continues to be the model which all others must follow, thus making nonsense of one of the "historic decisions" of the Twentieth Congress, to which some commentators at the time attached such importance.

The fact is that the concepts which we shall be examining are not only closely inter-related, but derive logically from the totalitarian nature of the communist creed. Certainly the assertion of principles does not necessarily mean that they will be enforced, or at least enforced with an equal degree of severity; and the present rulers may well have decided to apply them with a greater laxity, at least for the time being. But there is no indication that they intend to disavow them, nor can they do so without undermining their own position. Whether the internal situation in the Soviet Union will render necessary a larger degree of liberalism it is impossible to say. But if it does, we may expect a continuance of what is going on today, that is, a sort of rear-guard action in which the ruling clique permit activities they would earlier have condemned, while reserving the right to change their policy should this be "politically desirable". Such a policy leaves the fundamental principles unaffected and its adoption under one set of circumstances offers no assurance that it will be pursued under another.

I have reason to be grateful to many persons for their assistance, and in particular to Dr George Katkov, Mr Max Hayward, Mr E. E. Orchard, and Colonel G. E. Wheeler. I am under an especial obligation to Mr Wolfgang Leonhard, who not only read the whole manuscript, but whose knowledge of communist ideology, acquired as a former student at the highest training establishment of the Comintern, was of great value to me.

R. N. CAREW HUNT

St Antony's College,
  Oxford.
    December, 1956

AGGRESSION

S. E. Ozhegov's *Dictionary of the Russian Language* defines aggression as "The armed attack by one or several imperialist countries against other countries with a view to the occupation of their territories, their forcible subjugation and the exploitation of their peoples". Similarly, the *Large Soviet Encyclopædia* explains that it is a typical phenomenon of class-divided societies, and that it reaches its climax in imperialist countries, of the foreign policy of which it is the principal instrument. Of this policy the Atlantic Pact of 1949 is cited as an example.

Thus aggression can be predicated only of imperialist Powers, which is in line with the distinction made in communist theory between "just" and "unjust" wars, the former being wars waged by the Soviet Union for the purpose of "liberating" oppressed countries and imposing Communism upon them, and the latter wars waged by the imperialist Powers against each other or against the Soviet Union.

That aggression is permissible if it promotes the revolutionary cause was explicitly laid down by Lenin. In his *Bellicose Militarism and the Anti-Militarist Tactics of Social Democracy* (1908) he insisted that:

> "Obviously . . . it is not the offensive or the defensive character of the war, but the interests of the class struggle of the proletariat, or rather the interests of the international movements of the proletariat, that represent the only possible point of view from which the question of the attitude of

Social Democracy towards a given phenomenon in international relations can be considered".

Again, in *The Proletarian Revolution and the Renegade Kautsky* (1918) he declared that, "The character of a war (whether reactionary or revolutionary) is not determined by who the aggressor was, or whose land the 'enemy' has occupied. It is determined by the class which is waging the war, and the politics of which the war is the continuation". As the Soviet Government has identified its interests with those of world revolution, it has never scrupled, when it suits these interests, to attack countries with which it has signed pacts of non-aggression, as it had done, for example, with Poland and the Baltic States.

Further, the definition of aggression incorporated into the Convention signed in London on July 3rd 1933 between the Soviet Union and a number of countries, including Poland and Turkey, which was based upon the definition contained in the Politis Report to the Committee on Security Questions of the preceding May 24th, specifically laid down that aggression was not justified by "the internal condition of a State, e.g. by its political, economic or social structure; alleged defects in its administration; disturbances due to strikes, revolutions, counter-revolutions or civil war". Yet the Soviet Government has not hesitated to use such pretexts either for intervening itself, or for using its satellites to do so.

The justification for this is the principle that as socialist States are by their very nature incapable of aggression, no military action they take can be defined as such. This is a feature of communist thinking that we shall repeatedly encounter—the framing of definitions in such a way that the desired conclusion follows from them. To say that socialist States cannot commit aggression because they are non-aggressive is to utter a tautology, nor can there be any reason why they should possess this peculiar quality.

2

AGITATION

OZHEGOV'S *Dictionary of the Russian Language* defines agitation as "Oral and written activity among the broad masses which aims at inculcating certain ideas and slogans for their political education and for attracting them to the solution of the more important social and political tasks". Its direction is one of the functions of the Agitation and Propaganda (Agit-Prop) Department of the Central Committee of the C.P.S.U. Communist theory, however, draws a distinction between the two, this being based on the definition of Plekhanov that "a propagandist presents many ideas to one or a few persons; an agitator presents only one or a few ideas, but presents them to a mass of people". In his *What is to be Done* (1902), Lenin accepts this, and takes as an example the treatment of unemployment. A propagandist would give the reasons for it—that is, he would point out that it arises as a result of those recurrent crises which are inevitable under the capitalist system, the causes of which he would then go on to explain; whereas an agitator would choose some easily comprehended fact—e.g. that an unemployed worker's family had died of starvation—and use it to drive home to his hearers the single point that under Capitalism poverty exists in the midst of plenty. He would not attempt to explain why this should be so, as his object would be to arouse discontent and indignation.

Thus Lenin pointed out that the qualities of the propagandist and the agitator are not the same, but that their functions are complementary. In his *Left-Wing Communism* he says that when it is a question of winning over the vanguard of the proletariat to Communism, propaganda takes the first place, but that when it becomes one of aligning "all the class forces *for the final* and decisive battle, propaganda alone, the mere repetition of the truths of 'pure' Communism", is of no avail, because in such circumstances one must not count up to a thousand, as the propagandist does, but "in millions and tens of millions".

More generally, however, the task of the agitator is to direct mass opinion. He has to "sell" to the factory and collective farm workers whatever may be the party line, and secure their active collaboration in carrying it out. They cannot be expected to understand at all fully the principles of Marxism–Leninism, but they must be imbued with its spirit, so that they will be prepared to make the sacrifices demanded of them. For this purpose the Agit-Prop Department publishes a fortnightly *Agitator's Notebook*, which sets out the particular themes to be expounded and justified. Thus the agitator may have to explain why the production norms have been increased and working hours have been lengthened; or why there is such a shortage of consumer goods, despite official statements that the supply of them has increased. The part played by the agitator is therefore an extremely important one, as he is the link between the party leadership and the masses, and it is upon his success that the loyalty of the latter to the former will largely depend.

3

BOURGEOISIE

NEITHER Marx nor Engels were at much pains to state the meaning of the terms they used, and although the *Communist Manifesto* deals at great length with the misdeeds of the bourgeoisie, it was not until the English edition of 1888 appeared that Engels supplied a footnote which defined it as

4

"the class of modern capitalists, owners of the means of social production and employers of wage labour". In their writings it is identified with the new middle-class which the Industrial Revolution had brought into existence. Thus in his preface, dated March 15th 1845, to the *The Condition of the Working-Class in England*, which was first published in German, Engels explains that he has throughout "used the word *Mittelklasse* in the sense of the English word *middle-class*", which, "like the French word *bourgeoisie*, means the possessing class, specifically that possessing class which is differentiated from the so-called aristocracy". It is the class that has property, as opposed to the propertyless proletariat, so that, in Lenin's definition, "the bourgeoisie are all the owners of property".[1] Only, by Marx's day, property was coming increasingly to mean the possession of capital in the form of businesses, factories and the like as opposed to the possession of land, and thus the term bourgeoisie was used for capitalists in this sense, as it is today.

As the bourgeoisie was the creator of the capitalist system which Communism is pledged to destroy, the term is used pejoratively. At the same time, Marx and Engels admit, as their dialectic of history obliged them to do, that the bourgeoisie had been in its day a revolutionary class because it had challenged the decaying feudal economy, and that it had been responsible for an unparalleled leap forward of the productive forces. Their case, as set out in the *Manifesto* and elsewhere, was that it had fulfilled its mission, as it had become evident that it could no longer control the forces it had called into existence, and was acting as a "fetter" upon their further development. When this became evident is not, however, stated.

Further, Marx and Engels recognized the existence, at least in Western Europe, of a "liberal bourgeoisie", whose members were prepared to make certain concessions to the workers.

[1] *The Rural Poor* (1903), S.W., II, p. 236.

They imply that this "liberalism" cloaks, consciously or unconsciously, the realization that if the capitalist system was to continue, the worst abuses connected with it would have to be redressed; and as both were convinced that the system was irremediable, they regarded reforms within its framework as at best no more than palliatives. Nevertheless they held that the proletariat should ally itself with such liberal elements with a view to strengthening its position and enabling it ultimately to seize power. But in his speech at the Nineteenth Congress of October 1952, Stalin denied that such elements any longer existed:

> "The bourgeoisie used to allow itself to play the liberal, used to uphold bourgeois democratic freedoms and thereby gained popularity for itself among the people. Now not a trace of liberalism remains. The so-called 'freedoms of the individual' no longer exist—the rights of the individual are now accorded only to those who possess capital, while all other citizens are considered human raw material, fit only for exploitation".

When Lenin had sought to justify the regime set up after the revolution, he had denounced liberal democracy in equally fanatical language. But Stalin's presumed object in employing it was to indicate that the time had come to intensify the class struggle, and that Communist Parties were no longer to attempt to co-operate with the so-called "progressive bourgeoisie"—a line which was reversed at the Twentieth Congress of February 1956.

In present communist usage the term bourgeoisie is given, however, such an extension as to include all those who, whether they possess capital or not, have an interest in preserving the capitalist system which makes them opponents of Communism, and who develop an ideology which, for all its pretensions, is no more than the expression of this interest. This ideology survives their destruction as a class, and one of the main functions of a communist regime is to eradicate all traces of it, though why such "bourgeois survivals" should constitute a danger to society if the communist system is all that it claims to be, we are not told.

4

BOURGEOIS DEMOCRACY

BOURGEOIS democracy is a concept which goes back to Marx and Engels, though neither of them employ this precise term as Lenin and Stalin do, the former particularly in *The State and Revolution* (1917) and *The Proletarian Revolution and the Renegade Kautsky* (1918). Briefly, the thesis is that the contradictions within the capitalist economy bring into existence the bourgeois democratic State (or republic, as Lenin generally calls it) which is based on parliamentary institutions, and above all on the party system. As its power weakens, the bourgeoisie finds itself compelled to make concessions to the masses in the form of extensions of the suffrage, the recognition of freedom of the press and of association etc. But whereas its conservative section will resist such concessions as long as it is able, its liberal section will recognize their necessity and press for them. It is from this division of opinion that derives the party system, which is the hall-mark of bourgeois democracy, though Communists regard the conflicts between such parties as sham battles, because they take place within the framework of the capitalist economy, which neither party is prepared to abolish. The more the bourgeois democratic form of government develops, the more does it become the symbol of Capitalism in its decline. It represents what Marx calls "the political form of revolution of bourgeois society" as contrasted with its "conservative" form, and both

7

he and Engels hold that it is "the last form of bourgeois domination, that in which it is broken to pieces".

When therefore Lenin, who was in full agreement with the above, declared in his *Two Tactics of Social Democracy in the Democratic Revolution* (1905) that "Our party can only come into power in the form of the democratic republic", he did not mean that this type of parliamentary or party government would be adopted in the future socialist society, but simply that it was the form under which the bourgeois-democratic revolution, which would precede the proletarian revolution, must be carried out. Once the proletarian revolution had occurred, it would disappear, and "parliamentarianism" (*q.v.*) with it, and be succeeded by a higher form of popular representation which he called "proletarian democracy" (*q.v.*).

In fact communist writings, and especially those of Lenin, are filled with denunciations of the limitations and inadequacy of bourgeois democracy. The train of reasoning is perfectly logical once the premises are conceded. In capitalist countries the bourgeoisie is the dominant class, and bourgeois democracy is simply the political form which its domination takes. Hence, whatever the concessions the bourgeois-democratic State may make, it cannot be democratic, since to admit that it was would be to assert that democracy—i.e. the "rule of the people"—can be achieved under the domination of its "class enemy", which would be absurd.

In *The Proletarian Revolution* Lenin admits, however, that bourgeois democracy constitutes "a great advance in comparison with mediævalism" (whatever "mediævalism" with its infinite variety of social and political forms may mean), but that under Capitalism it is "false and hypocritical, a paradise for the rich and a snare and deception for the poor", since the capitalists "by a thousand and one tricks keep the masses away from the work of administration, and frustrate the freedom of

8

the Press, the right of assembly etc.", and bourgeois parliaments "*never decide* the most important questions, because they
are decided by the Stock Exchange and the banks". Thus he
contends that the political rights and freedoms conceded to
non-bourgeois elements are formal only, and have no real content. This was quite untrue, as Lenin, who had enjoyed for
years the protection of bourgeois governments, must have
been well aware; but he had somehow to justify the regime
set up in the Soviet Union, and as the term "democracy" has
a sort of talismanic value, he was not prepared to admit that
his revolution had destroyed it.

That bourgeois democracy is formal only is accepted, however, by all Communists, and this leads to a certain confusion in
their thinking, since if the rights and freedoms it confers have
no meaning because the bourgeoisie alone derive benefit from
them, it is not clear why their acquisition should assist the
proletariat in its struggle for power. However, in any discussion
upon the nature of democracy, Communists invariably seek to
minimize their importance. Thus at the conference on the
subject organized by Unesco in 1951, one speaker declared that
in the first half of the nineteenth century it was assumed that if
the masses secured political rights they would also secure political power. The 1848 revolutions demonstrated that this was an
illusion, and that the propertied class could concede the one and
retain the other. In consequence, the conservatives became
democrats, while the democrats widened the concept of
democracy from its political to its economic content. Similarly,
it was argued by a second speaker that by the time British
democracy had been enlarged into universal suffrage it was too
late, as "monarchy, trusts, monopolies, imperialism and an
imperialist foreign policy were already established".

Yet from one point of view the communist case is unassailable. It has been pointed out often enough that the party

system, which constitutes the essence of bourgeois democracy, is possible only as long as the parties are in general agreement as to the basis on which their society rests and conduct their political activity within its terms of reference. But as soon as a party arises which demands that the entire social, political and economic structure of society be changed, and which holds itself to be infallible and is not prepared to compromise or to admit that there is any common ground between it and other parties, the system naturally breaks down. This was Lenin's position, as it was implicitly that of Marx—a sworn enemy of parliamentary government. And, granted their premises, it is a logical one. For if society consists of two classes only—the exploiting capitalists and the exploited workers—each of which has its own interests, which are antagonistic to those of the other, and if the goal of history is the victory of the workers and elimination of their oppressors, there can no longer be any room for political parties once this goal has been achieved, seeing that all power will now belong to a single class whose members possess *ex hypothesei* a common will and interest.

5

BOURGEOIS NATIONALISM

ACCORDING to Lyekhin and Petrov's *Dictionary of Foreign Words*,

"Bourgeois nationalism or bourgeois-democratic nationalism, though acknowledging the equality of nations, always strives for the priority of its own, and seeks to obtain profits for itself, that is, for its national bourgeoisie. It strives for the division of nations, and for the development of national exclusiveness. As such, the party of Lenin and Stalin has always resisted it".

To bourgeois nationalism is therefore opposed "proletarian internationalism" (*q.v.*).

The theory developed by Lenin and Stalin taught that national States are the product of revolutions carried out by the bourgeoisie, and that since these revolutions were undertaken against feudalism, the bourgeoisie was acting as a revolutionary class, though it was at the same time seeking its own interests, which were to get rid of feudal particularism and establish a national market able to compete with that of other nations. The bourgeoisie would thus appeal to its own "native folk", and would persuade them that they too had an interest in promoting the national movement, which was true in so far as it is always desirable that feudalism be replaced by an economy which will develop the productive forces of society more efficiently. But the masses who rallied to the national cause were speedily disillusioned. They believed that they would belong to the nation, whereas they found themselves exploited, seeing that the victory of bourgeois nationalism is in fact that of Capitalism, since, as Stalin puts it, "a nation is an historical category belonging to a definite epoch, the epoch of rising capitalism". As soon as the victory over feudalism had been won, the class character of the revolution became apparent, and the bourgeoisie ceased to be revolutionary and became counter-revolutionary.

The objective characteristics of the nation find their subjective counterpart in national sentiment—the memory of "old, forgotten, far-off things and battles long ago"—and of this sentiment national flags, anthems and the like are the symbols. The worker is instinctively prepared to defend his own nation, as the domination of his own bourgeoisie is less unendurable than that of another. The national chauvinism of the bourgeoisie sedulously cultivates this sentiment, and whenever its

II

interests are threatened, as they come increasingly to be in the period of imperialism, it will appeal to "social patriotism", and, abetted by the Social Democrats, will egg on the workers of its own country against those of others in the name of so-called "national interests". But the class-conscious section of the proletariat has now become aware of the deception. It sees that the nation is only a phase, that under bourgeois national-ism liberty, fraternity and equality can never be realized, and that only under Communism will all peoples live peaceably side by side, developing their native cultures in complete freedom, and be protected by their common fatherland, the Socialist Soviet Union.

Bourgeois nationalism thus stands for any expression of national sentiment which is opposed to this consummation. As the *Political Dictionary* declares, it "blunts the idea of the class struggle between the oppressed and the exploiters in order to subordinate the workers to the influence of the bourgeoisie". Those who support it are thus "agents of the bourgeoisie who utilize national differences between peoples in order to inflame enmity between the working masses of the various nations in the interests of the bourgeoisie"—activities which are repre-sented as directed by foreign intelligence agencies with the object of restoring Capitalism in the Soviet Union and destroy-ing the fraternal unity which exists there. But current propa-ganda also ascribes to it any manifestation of public opinion which has the effect of welding together the various sections of society, thus weakening the struggle which the proletariat should be conducting against its national bourgeoisie and the solidarity it should feel with proletarians of other countries, and retarding the development of world revolution. More specifically, it stands for the refusal of a nation to accept the dictation of the Soviet Union, and its adoption of policies opposed to Soviet interests.

The position was clearly stated by Georgi Dimitrov at the Seventh Comintern Congress of 1935:

"We Communists are the *irreconcilable opponents on principle* of bourgeois nationalism in all its forms. But we *are not supporters of national nihilism*, and should never act as such. The task of educating the workers and all working people in the spirit of proletarian internationalism is one of the fundamental tasks of every Communist Party. But anyone who thinks that this permits him, or even compels him, to sneer at all the national sentiments of the wide masses of working people is far from being a genuine Bolshevik, and has understood nothing of the teaching of Lenin and Stalin on the national question".

What this meant was that national sentiment should be encouraged as long as it was directed against "feudal survivals" or against the national bourgeoisie, but was to be condemned as soon as it conflicted with the interests of the Communist movement or of the Soviet Union. Thus the charge of bourgeois nationalism was one of those most frequently brought against the Yugoslav Communists, who were accused in the Cominform Resolution of supposing that they could "build up Socialism without the support of the Communist parties of other countries, without the support of the Soviet Union". The defection of Tito was followed, in fact, by a violent campaign against it, as exemplified by a leading article in the *Cominform Journal* of December 1st 1948, which called it "the well-tried, poisonous weapon of imperialist reaction".

The "Theses on the National and Colonial Question", approved by the Sixth Comintern Congress of 1928, provide the most complete statement of the attitude to be adopted towards the national bourgeoisie, and thus towards bourgeois nationalism, in the struggle against imperialism in backward countries. Their tone is bitter, doubtless because the Russians were still smarting under the recent "betrayal of the revolution" by the Chinese national bourgeoisie; and thus, although it is admitted that this class has a certain importance which should not be under-rated, it is pointed out that it is powerless to achieve national independence, on account of the radical contradiction between it and its imperialist oppressor. Hence such independence can be won only by the proletariat under the leadership of the Communist Party.

Unfortunately for the theoreticians, there has been no case of a successful national liberation movement conducted upon these lines. At the same time, a number of Asian countries did recover their independence in the years immediately following the last war, but as they did so under non-communist leadership, and proceeded to set up governments in which the local Communist Party was not represented, Moscow refused to admit that they were genuinely independent, and declared their rulers to be "vassals of western imperialism". After Stalin's death, however, the Malenkov Government launched a new policy of gestures of friendship towards these uncommitted countries and of offers of technical assistance; and in the course of 1955 it became clear that the earlier position was being abandoned, as indeed it had been by the time of Krushchev's and Bulganin's Asian tour. Thus *Sovetskoye Vostokovedeniye* No. 1 of 1956 explains that the "unquestionably correct proposition" that the proletariat may (*sic*) become the leader in a "national liberation and anti-feudal movement" had led to the "incorrect deduction that only such leadership" could ensure victory in a struggle for national independence, with the result that when India, Burma, Indonesia and Egypt, where the proletariat was unable to play the leading role, won their independence under the leadership of the national bourgeoisie, the duality of the nature of that class was not appreciated, and it was wrongly portrayed as "the ally of imperialism in its struggle against the working masses". The meaning of this revaluation is that it is now recognized that such rulers as Colonel Nasser have their uses, even if their governments are not proletarian.

The present position is therefore that the struggle for national independence falls into two stages. In the first, the objective is *political* liberation from the imperialist power, and this, it is implied, need not be carried through under the leadership, or even with the participation, of the Communists, though it will owe its inspiration to the victorious struggles of the Soviet Union and of Communist China. The second stage is the pursuit of *economic* liberation under some form of State control, and this will be assisted by capital equipment and technical aid supplied by the socialist countries. It is assumed, however, that at some point in this process of industrial development the transition from Capitalism to Socialism will begin, and when this happens, the Communist Party *must* assume the leadership. Until this occurs, the role of the Communists will depend on circumstances, but they are, in general, to align themselves with "progressive" elements in order to bring pressure to bear on the government to carry out a forward social policy, and to attack all "survivals of imperialism", that is, any policy calculated to bring the country into the western orbit.

But within the Soviet Union it has never been to the advantage of the leadership to tolerate bourgeois nationalism, and any manifestation of it has been relentlessly crushed. Thus the "Theses of the Central Committee of the C.P.S.U.", issued on the occasion of the three hundredth anniversary of the incorporation of the Ukraine, and published in *Pravda* of January 12th 1954, contained, in addition to much falsification of history, an attack on Ukrainian bourgeois nationalism, reinforced by a quotation from Lenin to the effect that the country's only hope of independence lay in its association with Russia. The Ukranian poet Sosyura's *Love the Ukraine*, which had been at first highly commended, was eventually condemned on the grounds that it contained no reference to the blessings of such association and was a panegyric of everything Ukrainian. The same fate befell the epic poems of the Central Asian republics, which were suppressed as products of their native cultures, and as thus constituting an obstacle to the policy of Russification, though some of these have since been rehabilitated. As, however, bourgeois nationalism allegedly no longer exists in the Soviet Union, the question of a new attitude towards it does not presumably arise.

6

BUREAUCRACY

BUREAUCRACY in the sense of "officialdom" has always been regarded as objectionable, but in the Soviet Union the objection to it takes a peculiar form. Lyekhin and Petrov's *Dictionary of Foreign Words* defines it as "The system of government of the bourgeoisie through the medium of privileged persons divorced from and dominating over the masses". Similarly, bureaucratism is "an inclination towards a formal approach to any problem, which does not consider it as one that deals with human beings". As communist theory teaches that the bourgeois State only exists to promote the interests of the bourgeoisie and to exploit the masses, the same must be true of bureaucracy as the instrument it employs for this purpose, and thus to attack the one is to attack the other. At the same time it is recognized that bureaucracy is a danger to which even communist organizations are subject, and thus the *Short History of the C.P.S.U.* (*b*) declares that "a party perishes . . . if it allows itself to become covered with bureaucratic rust".

In fact it was inevitable not only that a bureaucracy should arise in the Soviet Union, but also that it should proliferate, seeing that under a communist regime every branch of the economy and form of social expression is subjected to official control. Yet although this development was the logical consequence of all that Lenin stood for, he took violent exception to it, as bureaucracy was associated in his mind with Tsarism, which was nothing if not bureaucratic, whereas he held that the characteristic of proletarian as opposed to bourgeois democracy was that it brought the masses into direct participation in the work of government. He had no experience of administration, and his ideas on the subject at the time of the revolution were of an almost unbelievable naivety. Yet although he found himself obliged to modify them, he never wholly abandoned his vision of a State which the workers would administer for themselves, albeit under the guidance of the Party, and the remedy for the evils of bureaucracy most commonly put forward has always been that their participation should be made more effective.

Lenin's forebodings were justified, as the new official class which arose after the revolution early developed the same defects as the class it had replaced. To these defects attention was drawn at successive Party Congresses, as for example, at the Nineteenth Congress of 1952, when Malenkov, referring to Stalin's past strictures, declared that bureaucracy meant the issue of unnecessary orders and decisions, and the absence of adequate measures to ensure the execution of such as were necessary, and demanded that there should not only be "verification from above" but also "from below"; that is, that the masses should be encouraged to report if any directive remained a dead letter.

It is of interest to note in passing that "verification from below" was one of Lenin's pet ideas, and led to the creation in

1919 of the Workers' and Peasants' Inspectorate (Rabkrin), which was to overhaul the entire official machinery and expose corruption and red tape. As Isaac Deutscher had pointed out, the cure proved worse than the disease, and the Inspectorate became an additional source of muddle and intrigue, as Lenin was later to discover.[1] Yet there was one man who profited by it. Stalin had been appointed its Commissar, and he thus acquired a control over the government apparatus, soon to be extended to that of the Party, which was the foundation of his rise to power. Malenkov's reference to it may not therefore have been made without intention.

In theory, bureaucracy is a bourgeois phenomenon, and thus does not exist within the Soviet Union. As the *Large Soviet Encyclopædia* asserts, the Soviet system of government makes such a state of affairs impossible by attracting the workers into the task of governing, though it then devotes half a column of close print to listing the various anti-bureaucratic measures taken by the Government at one time or another.[2] But Lenin always insisted that the administrative apparatus he had been obliged to set up did not constitute a bureaucracy, and Stalin, who enormously increased it, did the same. The stock argument has been that party and government officials are bureaucrats only if they behave as such. But it is freely admitted that they tend to do so, and if their administration leads to resentment, it is assumed that this is due to their failure to maintain that contact with the masses which is supposed to distinguish the Soviet functionary from his bourgeois counterpart. Attacks upon bureaucracy are therefore permitted, and even encouraged, as it provides a convenient scapegoat for the Soviet system of government which is responsible for it.

[1] Stalin (1949), pp. 230–1.
[2] Barrington Moore, Jr., *Soviet Politics: The Dilemma of Power* (Harvard 1951), p. 172.

CADRES

LYEKHIN and Petrov's *Dictionary of Foreign Words* defines cadres as "the basic establishment of workers in any undertaking or enterprise, party, or professional organization etc." The word is a French one, and means literally a "frame" or "framework"; but it has a technical meaning when applied to the army, which Littré gives as "L'ensemble des officiers et sous-officiers d'une compagnie", that is, those who have taken up soldiering as a profession as opposed to National Servicemen who have not, since in the French and other continental armies this is a necessary condition for obtaining officer or non-commissioned-officer rank. It is in the above sense that the term is used by Communist Parties to denote those who discharge a specific function, from the members of the central party organs down to the leaders of cells and those responsible for the work carried on in the various branches of the cell's activity. Thus the cadres are the effectives of the Party at any given time; and it was they whom Stalin had in mind when he told the graduates of the Red Army Academies in 1935 that "cadres decide everything", and when he declared in his Report to the Eighteenth Congress of 1939 that they constituted "the commanding staff of the Party". The term is similarly applied to the permanent establishment of any government organization or business enterprise; and at times, in a more restricted sense, to those whose higher educational standard raises them above the general level of their fellow workers, and qualifies them for inclusion in the managerial class.

In view of the importance of the party cadres, whom Stalin described in the above Report as its "gold reserve", the question of their selection has always been a major preoccupation. Stalin discussed this at the time; but he laid down no criterion, and apart from insisting that they must "become versed in the Marxist–Leninist science of the laws of social development", he contented himself with generalities to the effect that the merits and demerits of individuals must be studied, and that they should be given posts for which they possessed the necessary qualifications. It has long been accepted, however, that they must be selected on the basis, first of their political reliability, and secondly of their professional efficiency, a principle which Malenkov reaffirmed at the Nineteenth Congress, and which was incorporated into the revised Party Statutes (Art. III (k)). Malenkov may have been influenced by the fact that the policy of large-scale recruiting adopted during the war years had led not only to the admission of undesirable elements into the Party, but also to the appointment of cadres who had failed to justify the confidence reposed in them. None the less, the order is significant, and may in part explain why the cadres are so constantly criticized for their inadequacy, since, as political realiability implies something more than a general willingness to accept the party creed, men whose primary interest is in their professional competence are likely to be passed over. For as a *Pravda* editorial of August 4th 1953 put it:

"In their practical work of selecting and placing cadres, Party organizations proceed from the fact that selecting cadres correctly means selecting them, first, for political considerations, that is whether a particular official is worthy of political confidence, and secondly, for practical considerations, that is whether he is suitable for a particular job".

Indeed, no totalitarian regime can well adopt any other criterion. In his Report to the Twentieth Congress, Khrushchev was moved, however, by the interests of efficiency to insist that cadres should be so trained as to be able to combine

their party work with other forms of activity, and he stigma-
tized as "fundamentally wrong and harmful" the view held in
certain quarters that "party work is one thing and economic
and Soviet work quite another". Party schools should be so
reorganized that, "in addition to a thorough study of Marxist-
Leninist theory", students should acquire such practical knowledge of a definite branch of industry as was equivalent to a
"technical school standard", as he complained that specialization
in what was called "pure party work" was turning out
theorists and bureaucrats.

8

CAPITALIST ENCIRCLEMENT

FROM the moment they seized power, the Bolsheviks took it
for granted that they were encircled by enemies who would seek
to crush the "proletarian revolution" and the Soviet State with
which it soon became identified. As early as 1923 this conviction was given its theoretical expression in the preamble to
the U.S.S.R. Constitution, which laid down the doctrine of the
"two camps"—the capitalist and the socialist—which were
mutually antagonistic, and thus bound to come into collision.
As the former was represented by the bourgeoisie and the latter
by the proletariat (under the ægis of the Soviet Union), this
doctrine was no more than the extension to the international
plane of the class struggle which, according to Marx, could
only be resolved by some form of cataclysm.

Thus the invitation to the founding congress of the Comintern, drafted by Trotsky in January 1919, drew attention to the
danger that world revolution would be "throttled by the alliance of the capitalist States, which are banding together against
it under the hypocritical banner of the League of Nations".
In the same year, Lenin declared in *The Tasks of the Third*

International that "the bourgeoisie of the whole world, with all its might, with enormous energy, intellect and determination, stopping at no crime . . . is preparing to suppress the proletariat in the impending civil war"; while in his speech at the Third Comintern Congress of June 1921 he insisted that "the international bourgeoisie, full of fierce hatred and enmity, is ready at any moment to throw itself upon Soviet Russia and destroy it". Thus, however stable the international situation might appear, it was essentially a precarious one, and any change in it was calculated to lead to catastrophic results.

Stalin underlined the above. In an article of March 22nd 1925 on the international situation, he pointed out that "the mere existence of the Soviet State represents a mortal danger to imperialism".[1] In his *Problems of Leninism* (1926) he declared that "It should not be forgotten that as long as capitalist encirclement exists, so long will there exist the danger of intervention with all the consequences resulting from this danger". In *The Right Deviation of the C.P.S.U.* (April 1929) he asked, "For what purpose then does capitalist encirclement exist if not for international capital to employ all its strength to organize within our border areas rebellions of elements discontented with the Soviet regime?" Again, in his Report to the Sixteenth Congress of 1930 he said that "Capitalist encirclement is not simply a geographical conception. It means that around the U.S.S.R. there are hostile class forces, ready to support our class enemies morally, materially, by means of financial blockade and, when the opportunity offers, by means of military intervention."

Equally emphatic was the warning he gave the Central Committee on March 3rd 1937.

"They [i.e. some party members] forget that the Soviet Union is in a state of capitalist encirclement. . . . It is no

[1] *Soviet Documents on Foreign Policy* (ed. Jane Degras, 1951), I, p. 21.

empty phrase. It is a very real and unpleasant feature. It means that there is one country, the Soviet Union, which has established the socialist order in its own territories, and that alongside it are many countries which continue to carry on a capitalist mode of life, and surround the Soviet Union, waiting for an opportunity to attack it, to break it, or at any rate to undermine its power and weaken it".

He reiterated this in his much-publicized letter to Ivan Ivanov of February 12th 1938. "Only blockheads or masked enemies . . . can deny the danger of military intervention, at attempts at restoration, as long as capitalist encirclement exists". As a feature of these hostile machinations is held to be the sending into the country of spies, saboteurs and terrorists, it has long become the custom to ascribe the disgrace of leading party members to the discovery that they have been for years "agents of foreign intelligence services", and in this capacity have assisted such persons.

Any agreements concluded between capitalist Powers have been held to afford proof of their hostile intentions. Thus, in a press statement of August 5th 1928, Chicherin declared that the Kellogg Peace Pact, to which the Russians had not at that time been invited to adhere, was "clearly an integral part of the preparation for war against the U.S.S.R.",[1] this statement being in line with the imaginary "war scare" initiated without warning by Stalin in an article published in *Izvestiya* of July 28th 1927. To the same order of ideas belongs the notion, now a part of the Communist legend, that the policy which the Allied Powers pursued towards Germany in the inter-war years, including of course the Munich Agreement, was motivated by the desire to use that country to destroy Russia, so that Stalin declared in his *Economic Problems of Socialism in the*

---

[1] *ibid.*, p. 322.

U.S.S.R. (1952) that, "Of course, when the United States and Britain assisted Germany's economic recovery, they did so with a view to setting a recovered Germany against the Soviet Union, to utilizing her against the land of Socialism". The order in which the two countries is placed is of interest. In the inter-war years Britain was represented as the leader of this "Holy Alliance", as Stalin described it in his *Izvestiya* article in which he had explained that "English capitalism always has been, is, and always will be the most ferocious suppressor of popular revolutions".[1] After the setting up of the Cominform in September 1947 this role was transferred, as already noted, to the United States, of which it was claimed that Britain had now become a satellite.

Capitalist encirclement is one of the numerous terms in the communist vocabulary which can be described as "barometric", as the emphasis laid on it depends on how, at any given time, the Soviet Government views the outside world. During the first eighteen months after the Second World War it adopted a watchful but not entirely hostile attitude towards the West, and this was reflected in Stalin's statement to Alexander Werth of September 1946 that, "I do not believe that the ruling classes of Great Britain and the United States could create a 'capitalist encirclement' of the Soviet Union even if they wanted to do this, which however cannot be affirmed". It should be noted in passing that the operative word here is "ruling classes", which, according to communist theory, are necessarily reactionary in capitalist countries, and whose policies are assumed to be opposed to the wishes of the over-whelming majority of their peoples. But even as late as April 1947, by which time Soviet policy was moving towards the "cold war", Stalin made the surprising concession that the danger of capitalist encirclement no longer arose from the

[1] *Soviet Documents on Foreign Policy* (ed. Jane Degras, 1951), I, p. 234.

existence of capitalist States as such, but from their unwilling-
ness to co-operate with the Soviet Union; that is, from their
refusal to accept the manner in which the Soviet Government
was carrying out the obligations into which it had entered at
Yalta and elsewhere. After the establishment of the Cominform, however, Soviet relations with the Western Powers
sharply deteriorated, and the doctrine was unreservedly reaffirmed.

The Twentieth Congress of 1956 modified the Leninist
thesis that imperialism must inevitably lead capitalist States to
attack one another. But this does not affect the doctrine
of capitalist encirclement, which was not abandoned, nor
indeed can be as long as the Marxist dialectic is held to
provide the key to history. For if the dialectic possesses any
validity, Capitalism and Socialism must be regarded as opposed
forces—the one reactionary and the other progressive—and in
the conflict to which this antagonism leads, Socialism is
destined to prevail. The attempt of the capitalist world to
destroy its rival follows naturally from this. Yet it would seem
equally to follow that the socialist world is anxious to destroy
the capitalist world—a conclusion rendered at least plausible
by the activities of the Comintern and by Soviet foreign policy
generally. But Communist theory refuses to apply the principle
that it takes two to make a quarrel, as it is an axiom that the
Soviet Union, as a socialist State, is innocent of all hostile
intentions.

Apart from the above, the doctrine has also a practical value,
as it can be invoked to explain why the State, so far from
"withering away", becomes continually stronger, and to justify
the demands made upon the workers, who must be periodically
reminded of their perilous situation. The call for greater
"revolutionary vigilance" (*q.v.*) which accompanies such warn-
ings has a similar psychological effect, as the Soviet citizen is

led to believe that he is encompassed by enemies, and that his survival depends on his power to uncover their designs.

9

COEXISTENCE

IN proportion as the strength of the Soviet Union has grown, western public opinion has come to regard coexistence with it, or "peaceful coexistence" as it is often called, as increasingly desirable in the interests of world peace and as offering a solution of the present international tension.[1] But in the years immediately following the First World War it was the Russians who pressed for it, because they needed the assistance of capitalist countries to build up their internal regime. Thus the primary objective of Russian foreign policy was to break down the barriers which existed between the Soviet Union and the outside world by concluding trade agreements which paved the way for diplomatic recognition. In its note to the Western Allies of March 15th 1922 the Soviet Government declared that it was "under no illusion as to the fundamental differences that exist between the political and economic regimes of the Soviet Republics and that of the bourgeois states", but that it believed nevertheless that agreement on economic co-operation was possible;[2] and in stating the Russian case at the Genoa Conference of the following April, Chicherin went further, declaring that "in the present period of history, the Soviet Government desired diplomatic relations with the Governments . . . of all countries on the basis of . . . full and complete recogni-

---

[1] For an interesting discussion of this question see R. I. Aaron and P. A. Reynolds, "Peaceful Coexistence and Peaceful Co-operation" (*Political Studies*, Oxford, October 1956, pp. 283 f.), but although the distinction they make between the two doubtless exists, it is not recognized, at least explicitly, by Soviet theoreticians, who regard each as implying the other.
[2] *Soviet Documents on Foreign Policy* (ed. Jane Degras, 1951), I, p. 293.

tion".[1] Negotiations to this end broke down on the question of war debts. But with Germany, also ostracized at this time, agreement proved easier to reach, and the Rapallo Treaty of April 16th 1922 introduced the principle of coexistence; that is, of friendly relations between two countries with totally different economic structures.

Certainly the Soviet Union had everything to gain at this time by a policy of "appeasement". The writings and speeches of Lenin's last years contain repeated references to the advantages of peace and economic co-operation with the capitalist world; and the present Soviet leaders continually represent him as the apostle of coexistence, though what he understood by it was no more than the corollary of his belief that world revolution would be a gradual process. In an interview with the *New York Evening Journal* of February 18th 1920 he said, "Our plans in Asia? The same as in Europe: peaceful coexistence with the peoples, with the workers and peasants of all nations". The phrasing is significant as exhibiting the distinction, earlier noted, which Communists make between the masses, whose goodwill towards the Soviet Union is taken for granted, and the hostile "bourgeois governments" of their respective countries. Coexistence was thus in no way incompatible with the subversion of the latter, to which Communists were in principle committed. Nor did it imply any rejection of Marx's teaching. As Lenin pointed out in his Report to the Eighth Congress of March 1919, "The existence over any long period of the Soviet Republic side by side with imperialist States is unthinkable. One or the other must triumph in the end. And before that end supervenes, a series of frightful collisions will be inevitable". And again, "We must remember that we are at all times but a hair's breadth from every manner of invasion". In his defence in *Problems of Leninism* of the policy of

[1] *ibid.*, p. 298.

"Socialism in one country", Stalin made use of these statements. He added, "Clear, one would think!"

None the less, Stalin periodically asserted his belief in the possibility of coexistence. On September 9th 1927 he told the American Labour Delegation that "the existence of two opposite systems—the capitalist and the socialist—did not preclude temporary agreements", though they were limited by "the opposed character of the systems, between which there is rivalry and competition". For, according to his statement to the Fifteenth Congress of the following December, such coexistence would last only "until proletarian revolution ripens in Europe, or until colonial revolutions come fully to a head, or finally, until the capitalists fight among themselves". None the less, he told Walter Duranty in November 1930 that the very fact that the world had been at peace for ten years was a proof that coexistence was possible. Not that the Soviet Government could claim any credit for this. The policy of its Siamese twin, the Comintern, had never been more forcibly laid down than in the Theses of its Sixth Congress of 1928, which had set out the nature and purpose of the world revolutionary movement in the clearest terms, and had asserted that the Soviet Union was the centre of it.

But by the middle thirties Russia, now a member of the League of Nations, had achieved full international recognition, and was soft-pedalling its revolutionary activity in view of the danger of Germany. Thus on March 6th 1936, in reply to a question put to him by the American journalist Rex Howard, Stalin denied that the Soviet Union had ever sought to bring about world revolution, and said that "American democracy and the Soviet system could coexist and compete peacefully. . . . if we do not indulge in too much fault-finding over trivial things". But this was intended, as were his earlier utterances on the subject, for external and not for internal consumption, and in his letter to Ivanov of February 1938 he reverted to the Leninist thesis that coexistence over any prolonged period was an impossibility.

In the immediate post-war years, Stalin's views upon this subject were naturally canvassed upon numerous occasions. When Alexander Werth asked him in September 1946, "Do you believe in the possibility of a friendly and lasting collaboration between the Soviet Union and western democracy, despite the existence of ideological discord, and in friendly competition between the two systems?" he said, "I do, unconditionally!" Similarly, when Elliott Roosevelt asked whether it was possible for a nation such as that of the United States to live in peace with a communist form of government, he replied, "Yes: of course. This is not only possible; it is wise, and entirely within the bounds of realization." He used the same language in a reply to Harold Stassen in April 1947. The difference between the American and the Soviet economic systems was "not of essential importance where collaboration is concerned", and he pointed out that the fact that America and Germany had the same economic systems had not prevented them from going to war, whereas America had become the ally of the Soviet Union, which had an altogether different system. If collaboration was possible in time of war, why should it not be so in time of peace? He added, however, that there must be a genuine desire for it.

In Stalin's last years relations between the Western Powers and the Soviet Union progressively deteriorated, and his observations upon coexistence became less frequent and more guarded. His last pronouncement on the subject was in reply to a question put to him by a group of American editors, "On what basis is the coexistence of capitalism and Communism possible?", to which his answer, published in *Pravda* of April 2nd 1952, was that, "The peaceful coexistence of capitalism and

Communism is quite possible provided there is a mutual desire to co-operate, readiness to carry out undertaken commitments, and observance of the principle of equality and non-interference in the internal affairs of other States". These reservations were directly aimed at the policy of the Western Powers, and were presumably intended to be so understood.

Yet immediately after Stalin's death, the theme of coexistence re-emerged, and has since largely replaced peace as the main plank of Communist propaganda. On the day of the funeral Malenkov reaffirmed "Lenin's and Stalin's principle of the prolonged coexistence and peaceful emulation of the two different systems—the capitalist and the socialist", though Lenin had never admitted that it could be "prolonged", nor had Stalin done so in the inter-war years. At the session of the Supreme Soviet of August 8th 1953 he again declared that, "we stood and we stand for the peaceful coexistence of the two systems", and went on to say that "we consider that there is no objective ground for a collision between the United States and the Soviet Union", his meaning being that there was no essential reason why the two countries should collide, and that they would not do so provided that the former changed its policy. Again, in a speech to the Supreme Soviet of April 26th 1954, he pointed to "a certain relaxation of tension" which could be continued provided there was "peaceful co-operation among the nations, irrespective of their social structure". But the precondition of it was that all countries should carry out their obligations and cease to interfere in the internal affairs of other countries, which was simply to repeat what Stalin had said in April 1952, as recorded above, and his own statement at the Nineteenth Congress in which he had laid the entire responsibility for the existing tension upon the Western Powers.

But from at least 1955 there was evidence that the Soviet Government was moving nearer to the Titoist conception of "active coexistence", which meant, or professed to mean, accepting non-communist governments for what they were, and entering into normal relations with them. In an article in *Soviet State and Law* (No. 8, 1955), G. P. Zadorozhni said that there was no substance in the belief entertained by "certain circles in the West" that the absence of a common principle underlying the Soviet and the western concepts of international law rendered peaceful coexistence impossible. He insisted that coexistence had become a general principle of international law "at least from the date of the recognition of the Soviet Union by capitalist countries", and that, in addition to its legal aspect, it included "the development of comprehensive political, economic, social and cultural collaboration, or, more shortly, the ensuring of friendly competition in the course of which the question of the superiority of one of the two systems would be decided". He then gave numerous, if inconclusive, examples of measures recently taken by the Soviet Government to bring this about, which included "the friendly visit of Bulganin and Khrushchev to India, Burma and Afghanistan", though this had certainly not assisted the cause of peaceful coexistence as far as Britain was concerned.

This was only one of many articles which appeared at the time advocating peaceful coexistence, but pointing out that it did not imply any surrender to western standards. As Khrushchev told the East German Government delegation on September 17th 1955:

"The Soviet delegation at Geneva smiled, and that was not an artificial smile but a natural one. We honestly and sincerely desire friendly relations with all countries. But if anyone expects us to abandon our aims and our conviction that the teachings of Marx, Engels, Lenin and Stalin are correct, then he is making a serious mistake. We can only assure those who expect this that they will have to wait until Easter and Whitsun fall on the same day. We are honest men and always speak the truth. We say to you, our friends, as to our opponents: We are for coexistence because there are two social orders, social systems, in the world, Capitalism and Socialism. We suggest that peaceful competition will show which is right".

Similarly, he declared at the Twentieth Congress that:

"We cannot pass by the fact that some people are trying to apply the absolutely correct thesis of the possibility of peaceful coexistence of countries with different social and political systems to the ideological sphere. This a is harmful mistake. It does not at all follow from the fact that we stand for peaceful coexistence and economic competition with capitalism that the struggle against bourgeois ideology, against bourgeois survivals, can be relaxed. Our task is tirelessly to expose bourgeois ideology, reveal how inimical it is to the people, and show up its reactionary nature".

This hardly bodes well for peaceful coexistence. Yet Khrushchev could scarcely say less without jettisoning communist principles. Clearly the Soviet leaders have now decided that the policy of political and economic penetration can best be furthered if Communist Parties form alliances with other left-wing groups; and this is a wise decision, seeing that whenever the party line has moved to the left, these parties have been severely weakened, while whenever it has moved to the right, and Popular or National Fronts have been encouraged, they have gained in strength. It is therefore when the line moves to the right that other left-wing parties have most to fear, since the Communists will now appeal vociferously for working-class unity, and will accuse those who refuse to co-operate with them of opposing it. Yet the Communists have also to beware. Khrushchev may well insist that there is to be no compromising with principle. Yet whenever Communist Parties adopt a conciliatory attitude in an attempt to win mass support, they run the risk of losing their distinctive character, as they can increase their following only by diluting their programme. Moscow has always been aware of this danger, and this accounts for why a shift to the right has been followed after an interval by one to the left.

In view of the present line, it is, however, only natural that there should be much talk of peaceful coexistence. Yet if this is to be more than a matter of temporary convenience, each party must be prepared to accept the position of the other, however much it may disagree with it, as the Catholic and Protestant countries of Western Europe were led to do after the Wars of Religion had proved that however desirable unity of belief might be, it was unattainable. That the Soviet leaders have not yet learnt this lesson is abundantly clear.

10

COLLECTIVE LEADERSHIP

THE principle of collective leadership in the Russian Communist Party is not a new one. It derives, as E. H. Carr has pointed out, from the practice of the French Revolution, and although, as he says, it "did not figure in any of the party programmes and was not a prescribed item of party doctrine", it was none the less accepted as "according with the spirit of democratic Socialism that decisions should rest not with individuals but with the collective group".[1] In fact not even Stalin would have challenged its theoretical validity, however

[1] *The Bolshevik Revolution*, II, pp. 187–8.

much he may have ignored it in practice. After his death it was reaffirmed by his successors, just as it had been after the death of Lenin, though with far greater reason, as Lenin's predominance had been due to his personal authority, whereas Stalin's had rested upon terrorism.

Hence the new Soviet leaders lost no time in asserting that "collective leadership is the highest principle of party leadership", and this theme was elaborated in a lengthy article by L. Slepov, then editor of *Pravda*, which appeared in the issue of April 16th 1953. He pointed out that the Party had set itself to raise the standard of leadership, and to put an end to "administrative methods" which had been introduced during the war, when they had had a certain justification, but which had led to serious shortcomings. That all important principles should be decided upon collectively was a fundamental principle, and Stalin was quoted as having given, in 1931, the example of the Central Committee as a body peculiarly fitted to make decisions in this manner "as the wisdom of our party is concentrated in this Areopagus". For no matter how able the leaders may be, "they cannot replace the initiative and experience of the collective whole", and the decisions of individuals will always tend to be biased and one-sided. It is significant, however, that Stalin's decisions are not referred to as evidence of this, as they were later to be, but only those of such relatively unimportant persons as the First Party Secretary of the Dzhalal–Abad Provincial Committee.

Among the various malpractices associated with the failure to observe the principle of collective leadership are the taking of decisions without prior discussion; the holding of meetings of party committees at which only a minority of the members are present; or of meetings at which criticism is disallowed, seeing that "the function of collective leadership is to enable members to correct and criticize one another"; the basing of decisions upon questionnaires rather than upon open discussion; the failure to circulate in advance such material as members of a committee require if they are to be in a position to make a decision; and the altering of resolutions without the authority of those responsible for their original form. The above strictures are primarily aimed at Party Secretaries, who allegedly take the law into their own hands, thus exhibiting that "cult of personality" (*q.v.*) which it is the purpose of collective leadership to abolish.

An editorial in *Kommunist* of April 1956 condemns Stalin's rejection of collective leadership as "very harmful", and as having led *inter alia* to "violations of socialist legality". But it goes on to say that, under the cloak of attacking it, "certain rotten elements" are "attempting to cast doubts upon the party policy and its Leninist roots", and that its condemnation does not imply the rejection of the principle of "one-man management". This is developed further in an editorial in *Party Life* of the same month. It declares that "single-handed management without reliance on the collective fetters the independent action of the workers" and leads to an "excessive self-confidence" among the managers. But this, it hastens to add, is not to be taken as a repudiation of leaders and leadership. "Some people", it is stated, "have gone so far as to throw doubt on the right of the director of an enterprise to make the necessary transfers of workers, and impose fines for breaches of discipline and the like"—"anarchistic ideas" which the Party has very properly rejected. Apart from the above, the article evades the thorny problem of how collective leadership is to be applied to industry, and restricts itself to generalities about the right of members to take part in the discussion of party questions.

One point which is not, however, made clear is how, under collective leadership, decisions are actually arrived at. Presumably it is by a majority vote, in which event the minority will be expected to associate itself with the majority for the sake of party unity. For a minority to continue its opposition would be an offence against the centralist element in "democratic centralism", while any attempt to organize such opposition would be "fractionalism" (*q.q.v.*).

Reference should also be made to the practice revived by the Bolsheviks when they came into power, as it had in fact been introduced by Peter the Great, of attaching to every People's Commissar a Collegium of members of his Commissariat which he was required to consult before promulgating an order. The object of this was to prevent him from acting in an arbitrary manner by obliging him to submit his decisions to a body of experts. This practice fell into abeyance under Stalin, but his successors have returned to it as being in line with the collective leadership principle. But here again it is not proposed that its application should prejudice "one-man management", as a Minister may issue an order even if his Collegium does not agree with it, and although the latter may appeal against him to the Council of Ministers, it is unlikely to proceed to so drastic a step.

II

COSMOPOLITANISM

IN the 1935 edition of his *Dictionary*, D. N. Ushakov defined a cosmopolitan as "a citizen of the world", but by the time the 1949 edition of Ozhegov's dictionary had appeared, the meaning had changed to that of a traitor to his country. Similarly the 1952 edition of the *Short Philosophical Dictionary* declared cosmopolitanism to be "a reactionary theory that preaches indifference to the fatherland, to national traditions and to national culture". It is the opposite of nationalism, and "expresses the ideology and politics of the bourgeoisie".

"At present, it is cultivated by American imperialists who are striving for world-hegemony. It aims at inducing peoples to renounce their struggle for national independence and sovereignty and set up a 'world government' which will be at the service of imperialism. Just as chauvinism is being whipped up in the United States in order to prepare the American people ideologically for a war of aggression, so cosmopolitanism is being used to atrophy among other peoples any concern for the fate of their countries, to sap their patriotism, and make them docile instruments in the hands of the imperialists".

Thus the article goes on to declare that cosmopolitanism is used by "the Anglo-American imperialists" as a cover for espionage; that it is "supported by the right-wing Socialists—faithful valets of imperialism"; that it finds its expression in "the 'bandit's plan' known as the 'Marshall Plan' "; and that, more generally, "it manifests itself in the form of servility towards 'rotten bourgeois culture', disparagement of the great achievements of Soviet socialist culture, and contempt for the primary role played by the Russian people".

The term did not appear, however, in the Zhdanovite decrees on literature and the arts of 1946–7, and when G. F. Aleksandrov was attacked in the latter year for his *History of Philosophy*, it was of objectivism that he was accused. The Soviet leaders seem, indeed, to have been somewhat chary of giving it an abusive meaning, as to do so conflicted with the concept of internationalism. But in the second half of January 1949 the Twelfth Plenum of the Presidium of the Union of Soviet Writers decided to initiate a campaign against literary and dramatic critics charged with disparaging Soviet culture and "kow-towing to the West"; and this opened with an article in *Pravda* of January 28th in which cosmopolitanism was associated with international Jewry, Zionism, Pan-American-ism and Catholicism, and with an article in *Culture and Life* of January 30th. The principal offenders were declared to be the Jews, who had been attacked in the previous year as "rootless" (*bezrodnye*, lit. "without family"), a word used in the above article in the *Philosophical Dictionary*, though without specific reference to them.

During the war, many Russians had believed that they were fighting for values which transcended those for which their own particular society stood. In the view of the leaders, it was undesirable that they should continue to believe this. Hence the task of unmasking cosmopolitanism was entrusted to the well-known Soviet theoretician M. Mitin, and in two articles in the *Literary Gazette* of March 9th and March 12th 1949 twelve prominent intellectuals, five of whom were Jews, were accused of it. Among them was M. Rozenthal, co-editor, with P. Yudin, of the *Philosophical Dictionary*, who should thus know what he is talking about. Since Stalin's death the term has been less frequently used in Soviet propaganda, as the anti-semitic campaign was dropped, as was also the insensate glorification of everything Russian, with its consequent disparagement of whatever was not, attacks upon intellectuals abated, and the new leaders moved towards a policy of *détente* with the West. None the less, at the Second Congress of Soviet Writers in December 1954, its Secretary-General, Alexis Surkov, equated cosmopolitanism with "the repulsive ideology of the war-mongers"; and in a pamphlet published in January 1956 with the title *The Party's Fight for Lofty Ideology in Soviet Literature in the Post-War Period*, the author, L. A. Plotkin, declared that "Our press severely but justly condemned the critics who were guilty of cosmopolitan mistakes, who tried to deny the serious successes of Soviet art", and that "Fighting consistently and energetically against cosmopolitanism, the Party has always

82758

pointed out that it is the other side of bourgeois nationalism, and that both are survivals of bourgeois ideology and equally alien to the Soviet people".

Since the Twentieth Congress, attacks on cosmopolitanism have virtually ceased, though, as we have seen, it is still maintained that they were fully justified when they took place. But as late as November 1954 the danger to which it exposed Soviet literature was analysed by N. Gribachev in a lengthy article in *Kommunist*. He too complained of "the lack of a fundamental elaboration of Marxist–Leninist aesthetics", that is, of the failure to provide a normative standard by which works of creative literature are to be judged. Yet the doctrine of "socialist realism" (*q.v.*) so far supplies it inasmuch as it is within the meaning of this concept that the conflicts between situations and characters in a story must be exhibited, their nature depending on the stage of development that society has reached, so that in the Soviet Union they are now no longer antagonistic, thus presenting the writer with a harder problem than that with which he was faced when he could deal with them in terms of a clearly defined class struggle. Gribachev's indictment of bourgeois writers is not, however, that they ignore conflict, but that they fail to see that it arises from the nature of bourgeois reality itself; that they are content to record it dispassionately, thus falling into the error of "bourgeois objectivism" (*q.v.*); and that they hold that "man carries conflict within himself as an inherent imperfection of his nature", so that it is represented as something which arises out of the human situation, and not, as socialist realism teaches, from the constitution of society.

It is scarcely necessary to add that as long as the hunt for cosmopolitans was up, all Communist Parties took part in it. In articles in the *Cominform Journal* Georges Cogniot of the French Communist Party and Sikorsky of the Polish Workers'

PROPERTY OF UNITED STATES

Party both described cosmopolitanism as "the tactic of American imperialism". The Czech Communist, Vaclav Kopecky, declared that it "expressed a view widely held in bourgeois society that science is something higher than the nation, something belonging to the world as a whole", and that this had led to an attitude of servility towards western science. He complained that education had been similarly affected, so that Napoleon and Byron were exalted over far greater Russian generals and poets, while children were actually being taught that the highest mountain in Europe was Mont Blanc, whereas it was Mt. Elbruz in the Caucasus. The press of the western Communist Parties published similar absurdities.

12

CRITICISM AND SELF-CRITICISM

In listing the duties of party members, Art. 3(a) of the revised Party Statutes, adopted by the Nineteenth Congress of 1952, lays down that they are "To develop self-criticism and criticism from below, to expose and eliminate shortcomings in work, and to fight against a show of well-being and against being carried away by success in work. Suppression of criticism is a great evil. He who silences criticism and substitutes ostentation cannot remain in the ranks of the party". Art. 4(b) gives every party member the right to criticize any official at a meeting and to address statements or questions to any party body up to the Central Committee. Finally, Art. 28 declares that the party member has an "inalienable right to take part in free and businesslike discussions on questions of party policy in any individual party organization or in the party as a whole"; and that this right "stems from inner party democracy", on the basis of which alone can self-criticism be developed. This emphasis on the two is significant since, although their importance has always been recognized, no reference was made to them in the Party Statutes of March 1939.

Their ostensible object, as set out by Malenkov in his Report to the Congress, is (i) to stop complacency and self-satisfaction, which may easily develop into negligence and inefficiency, (ii) to expose defects in the various projects in the political and economic field, (iii) to prevent the Party and its governing officials from turning into a bureaucratic caste immune from criticism and cut off from the masses, and (iv) to obtain the active participation of the masses in the building up of the Soviet system, since "criticism from below reflects creative initiative and enterprise in millions of working people, and their concern for the strengthening of the Soviet State". Malenkov pointed out, however, that it was an error to suppose that "criticism from below" would develop spontaneously, as it would not take place unless those who came forward with "healthy criticism" were assured that they would be supported, and that steps would be taken to get rid of the defects to which they had drawn attention. That they have suppressed criticism is thus one of the charges most commonly brought against party officials who have fallen into disgrace. A similar line was adopted by the Twentieth Congress.

Criticism and self-criticism are normally treated as though they were one and the same thing, though there is in fact a distinction between them. Criticism denotes the duty of every party member to bring to the notice of the authorities anything which he regards as calculated to weaken the regime, and thus it ranges from the denunciation of individuals to complaints as to how some enterprise—e.g., a factory or collective farm—is being run, or as to the shortage or excessive cost of some essential commodity. Where, however, matters of policy are concerned, the doctrine of "democratic centralism" insists that a measure may be criticized only until a decision with regard to it has been taken by the competent authority, after which it is no longer permissible. Even so, Lenin laid down certain conditions. The criticism must be submitted for discussion to the Party (or party organization) as a whole, and not to groups. Further, it must take the form of a practical effort to rectify abuses, and the critic must bear in mind "the position the Party occupies in a ring of enemies". Thus while in theory the party member is permitted and encouraged to criticize, unwelcome criticism can easily be dismissed as "destructive" rather than "constructive", or it may be condemned as containing by implication an attack on the ideological basis of the Soviet order which lies outside the field of criticism altogether.

Self-criticism, on the other hand, is the duty of all who direct party organizations openly to admit shortcomings since, as the *Short History of the C.P.S.U.* puts it,

> "The history of the party teaches that a party cannot perform its role as leader of the working class if, carried away by success, it begins to grow conceited, ceases to observe the defects in its work, and fears to acknowledge mistakes and frankly and honestly to correct them in good time. A party is invincible if it does not fear criticism and self-criticism".

The original authority for this practice is the statement in Marx's *Eighteenth Brumaire* (1852) that a distinctive feature of proletarian as opposed to bourgeois revolutions was that the former continually criticize themselves.

> "Bourgeois revolutions, like those of the eighteenth century, storm swiftly from success to success . . . but they are short-lived . . . On the other hand, proletarian revolutions,

like those of the nineteenth century, criticize themselves constantly, interrupt themselves continually in their own course, come back to the apparently accomplished in order to begin it afresh, and deride with unmerciful thoroughness the inadequacy, weaknesses and paltrinesses of their first attempts".

Hence both before, and still more after, his party had seized power Lenin stressed its importance. "All revolutionary parties which have hitherto perished did so because they grew conceited, failed to see where their struggle lay and *feared to speak of their weaknesses.* But we shall not perish as we do not fear to speak of our weaknesses and will learn to overcome them". At the same time, it does not seem to have become a normal feature of party life until after the Kronstadt mutiny of 1921, which made it necessary for the Party seriously to take stock of its position. But the role henceforth assigned to it was doubtless connected with the decree of the Tenth Congress of April of the same year which condemned as "fractionalism" (*q.v.*) the formation of groups within the Party. Clearly some concession had to be made, since it was impossible, at least at that time, to silence opposition altogether, and this took the form of permitting criticism provided that it was so canalized as to make it possible to control.

There is no cause to doubt that criticism and self-criticism are believed to serve a useful purpose, and that the official explanations given above go some way to accounting for this. If, however, we enquire into the matter somewhat more closely, we may conclude it is also valued for the following reasons. First, it is always desirable that a dictatorship should provide some form of safety-valve, and if this at the same time gives the ruling clique an indication of the trend of popular opinion, so much the better. Hence criticism directed to pointing out shortcomings in the Soviet economy will certainly receive attention on the higher levels, and if it is found to reflect the views of a considerable cross-section of the community, it may lead to appropriate action.

Yet such criticism is not always as spontaneous as it would appear. One common form it takes is that of letters to the press, carefully channelled and directed by the Party, drawing attention, for example, to some piece of administrative incompetence that the authorities have decided to expose. This method serves the double purpose of scarifying the organization in question, while encouraging the illusion that the Party is ever ready to champion the grievances of the masses, of whom, albeit the vanguard, it is also allegedly the servant.

Secondly, while the over-riding consideration of the Russian party leaders is the maintenance and extension of their power, it is none the less true that they also desire, in accordance with what has always been their professed aim, to bring the masses into the work of administration, always of course with the proviso that the masses are prepared to accept their direction. It is clearly to their advantage that the administration should be as broadly based as possible, as not only would this make their own task an easier one, but it would also enable them to represent the regime as genuinely democratic. The problem they have always had to face is how to bring about this state of affairs without weakening their own position, and this is one with which they now appear to be seriously exercised. They want to stimulate criticism because they hold that it will produce a more co-operative type of citizen. At the same time, the rigid system of government which they have imposed over the years has created a number of "defence mechanisms", the conscious or unconscious operation of which makes it improbable that the ordinary citizen will venture to criticize any general feature of Soviet life, unless he knows that he is protected because the

44

criticism has already been made officially or has received official sanction. Indeed, in Stalin's lifetime criticism was virtually non-existent. To criticize higher authority was much too dangerous, and only the most courageous were prepared to stick their necks out by doing so. It is this resistance that the present Soviet leaders are now trying to break down; and at the meetings of cells and of the committees of cities, districts and provinces which were held, in accordance with the Party Statutes, before the Twentieth Congress took place, there seem to have been cases of genuine criticism. Yet fear of the consequences of such action has not yet been exorcised, and a recent number of *Krocodil* has a cartoon in which a large cat of terrifying aspect addresses a very frightened mouse with the words, "Well! You have made your complaint. And now, what is your defence?"

Thirdly, it assists the Party in its task of keeping under constant scrutiny the motives and behaviour of everyone who holds a responsible position. Margaret Mead maintains that it is assumed that any party member is capable at any time of betraying his trust;[1] and there may indeed be some justification for this belief, seeing that, human nature being what it is, a party which makes absolute demands can never be sure that they will be carried out, and has therefore to act upon this supposition.

Fourthly, it is held to promote efficiency. Anyone at all conversant with the ways of the world will be aware that it is often found convenient to hush up some policy or action which has proved a failure. Doubtless this occurs in Russia also. Yet criticism and self-criticism may none the less provide a certain safeguard, in so far as the former draws attention to mistakes which have been committed, while the latter obliges those responsible to admit that they have made them.

[1] *Soviet Attitudes towards Authority* (New York, 1951), p. 31.

Lastly, it has a psychological value as symbolizing the complete obedience that every official, however exalted, owes to the Party, to whose collective will he must submit. If therefore he has committed some action of which it disapproves, he must be prepared to have this pointed out to him and make public confession of his offence, and it is repeatedly emphasized that there is nothing derogatory in this, and that to accept it is indeed the mark of the good Communist. As we shall see, it may well be that his offence may simply be to have carried out faithfully a policy which has proved wrong, but with which he was charged by the very persons who are now criticizing him; but this is the price of membership of a monolithic party which cannot admit error, and he may reflect that he is only being paid in the same coin as he will have given to others at one time or another.

There are, however, certain situations which particularly impose the obligation of self-criticism. Thus there may be a power struggle in the C.P.S.U. itself, or between it and another Communist Party, as for example that of the Yugoslavs, or in some other party, such as that which took place in the French Communist Party between Jacques Duclos and André Marty. Such conflicts cannot be openly admitted for what they are, and have therefore to be represented as due to ideological divergencies, just as the controversy between Moscow and the Yugoslav Communist Party was soon promoted to this plane. We need not, however, be too cynical about this. Undoubtedly Communists do believe that there is a close connection between theory and practice, and this predisposes them to regard the clash of two rival personalities as a conflict between two opposed interpretations of the official doctrine, only one of which can be correct. In this event, the loser will have to admit his error, and by his act of self-criticism re-integrate the group. Provided that his good faith is not questioned, he will remain in the Party, and the worst he will suffer will be a demotion; whereas if he refuses to submit, he may well be discovered to have been an enemy agent and be expelled.

We are not called upon to enquire here into the various hypotheses that have been put forward to explain the statements elicited at the purge trials of the middle 'thirties, and on certain occasions in the post-war period, as such statements are not acts of self-criticism, but confessions of guilt, often in respect of crimes which the self-accuser cannot possibly have committed. Thus Beriya did not make a self-criticism, but simply a confession—at least, according to report. But the public disavowal by leaders of their policies, or by intellectuals of their opinions, commonly takes the form of a self-criticism, even though they are also recantations, as they have been imposed by a higher authority. It is, in fact, impossible clearly to distinguish between the two. All that can be said is that party members, when called upon to give an account of their stewardship, are required to criticize themselves, though the form this takes may be dictated by the fact that a specific charge has been brought against them. Doubtless there will be some who will attempt to carry it out sincerely, and indeed it may even become a form of masochism. Yet the insistence that it should be practised upon all occasions tends inevitably to degrade it to a routine exercise—a sort of "General Confession" which commits those who make it to no more than the admission that whatever they have done might have been done better. Examples of it may be found in the reports of leading members of Communist Parties which used to appear in every issue of the *Cominform Journal*. After recording in the first two-thirds the remarkable progress that has been achieved, they were required to devote the remaining third to the mistakes that had been committed and the defects that remained to be overcome; and this followed a set pattern, so that what any one of them had to say might have been said by any other. Insufficient attention had been paid to the selection of cadres, the political indoctrination of many members was still far from what it should be, and so the list went on.

While, however, criticism and self-criticism normally have the meaning set out above, they have also been interpreted in a wider sense. According to the dialectic, progress takes place only through the conflict and reconciliation of contradictions; and Marx had maintained that the particular contradiction which was the motive force behind the historical process was that created by the existence of antagonistic classes, that is, the class struggle. But in 1936 Stalin had announced that the "victory of Socialism" had been achieved within the Soviet Union, and that although classes continued to exist, they were no longer antagonistic. Hence the ideologists were faced with the problem of what replaced the class struggle as the motive force behind the dialectical movement of Soviet society, and at the conference of philosophers held in June 1947, Zhdanov declared that it was criticism and self-criticism:

"Our Party [he said] long ago discovered . . . that particular form of revealing and overcoming the contradictions of socialist society, for such contradictions exist and philosophy cannot avoid dealing with them . . . In our Soviet society, where antagonistic classes have been liquidated, the struggle between the old and the new, and consequently the development from the lower to the higher, proceeds not in the form of struggle between antagonistic classes and cataclysm, as is the case under capitalism, but in the form of criticism and self-criticism, which is the real motive force of our development. . . . This is incontestably a new aspect of movement, a new type of development, a new dialectical law".[1]

[1] *Pravda*, July 30th 1947.

This explanation continued to be advanced up to the death of Stalin, since when it would seem to have been abandoned in favour of the view that in a socialist (or communist) society the elements of conflict, albeit no longer antagonistic, are supplied by the contradiction between the productive forces on the one hand and their capacity to satisfy the demands made upon them on the other.

Again, the Soviet philosopher M. A. Leonov in a study on the subject published in 1948, identifies criticism and self-criticism with the critical faculty as such. Criticism (and self-criticism with it) is represented as the characteristic feature of Marxism–Leninism, which not only criticizes other world views, but also its own, condemning the former and seeking to actualize the latter. It is essential to that development of knowledge on which progress depends, and all the great discoveries of the past have been based upon it. Yet prior to Marx it had never been wholly scientific. The criticism of Kant and Hegel had ended in reactionary systems; and while that of the eighteenth-century French materialists was genuine, inasmuch as it strove for the advancement of science and opposed speculative philosophy, it was limited because it was not conceived as a practical revolutionary activity, with the result that its influence was restricted and did not touch the political struggle of the masses. Then at last Marx revealed the true nature of reality and of man as a part of reality, and at the same time provided, in the form of the dialectic, the only valid explanation of how changes in society come about. Thus he created a criticism which was completely scientific, as it rested for the first time upon objective truth. Hence it is the method which on the one hand exposes contradictions in the non-socialist world, and on the other enables those contradictions within society to be discerned and overcome.

13

CULT OF PERSONALITY

The cult of personality is the euphemism employed today for Stalin's crimes and blunders, or at least those which his successors, albeit involved in them, have found it convenient to disown. But before examining it in this particular connection it should be noted that it has a wider extension, as it is an expression of the view that history is made by so-called "great men", this being opposed to the classical Marxist doctrine which teaches that it develops according to a prescribed pattern determined by economic laws. To admit that it lies within the power of individuals, however eminent, to deflect it from its predestined course would be to introduce an accidental and fortuitous factor, and would even make it possible to argue that it may not, after all, end with the establishment of the classless society of Communism, which it is the whole object of "scientific Socialism" to show that it must do.

While therefore not denying the exceptional role that great men play, Plekhanov insists that they are the product of the social relations of their time, and arise in response to social needs.[1] As Engels puts it, if there had been no Napoleon, "another would have filled his place", for this, he says, "is established by the fact that whenever a man was necessary, he has always been found". He gives as further examples, Cæsar, Augustus and Cromwell.[2]

It will be observed that Engels does not simply say that a social need is the condition for the emergence of a great man whose exceptional ability makes him its spokesman, but contends

[1] *The Role of the Individual in History* (1898), Eng. trans. 1940, p. 53.
[2] Letter to H. Starkenburg, January 25th 1894, *Correspondence* (ed. Torr), p. 518.

that the social need is sufficient to ensure that such a man will be forthcoming. Yet, as Sidney Hook points out, this is to argue in a circle, since there is no means of determining whether or not he has arisen in response to such a need until after the event.[1]

Contemporary Soviet theory represents the cult of personality as a principle of Narodnik (and later of Social Revolutionary) doctrine, which Plekhanov is held to have exposed. According to it, history is made by "heroes" and the masses are an inert "mob". In fact, Lenin understood it in this sense, and his objection to the individual acts of terrorism carried out by the Narodnik left-wing and by the Social Revolutionaries was not, as he himself explains, due to any moral scruple, but to his belief that such acts engendered a passive attitude in the masses by encouraging them to suppose that the revolution would be won without their participation. This charge is revived in *Party Life* of March 1956, though with a certain shift of emphasis, to provide a historical justification for condemning the Stalinist cult of personality: "The Marxist role of the individual in history was worked out in the struggle against the reactionary theses of the 'hero' and the 'mob', opportunist theories of elemental development and spontaneity that deny the role of the Party and its leaders in the revolutionary movement."

The attack on the cult of personality, as reflected in Stalin's autocratic rule and in the repeated assertions that he was supreme in every field of creative activity, gathered impetus after the Twentieth Congress, and was taken up in one Soviet journal after another in order to show its baneful effects in the particular field in which the journal in question had an interest. An unsigned article of exceptional violence in *Young Communist* of February 1956 declared that it had led to the complete suppression of the Komsomol as an independent

[1] *The Hero in History* (New York, 1950), pp. 79-80.

organization; *Questions of Philosophy* of April complained that it had had the effect of limiting the study of the problems of dialectical and historical materialism to those which Stalin had dealt with in his writing devoted to this subject, and to a consequent neglect of the works of Marx, Engels and Lenin; while *Soviet Pedagogics* of September dwelt upon its malign influence on the young, observing *inter alia* that the introduction of compulsory elementary education had been represented as due to Stalin's "fatherly solicitude", whereas it had in fact been rendered necessary by the development of Soviet society. The last-named periodical refers to the important directive of the Central Committee of June 30th, "On eliminating the cult of personality and its consequences", the text of which was published in *Pravda* of July 1st, one object of which is stated to have been to meet the charge that the cult had arisen from the nature of the Soviet system, whereas it is to be attributed to "certain conditions which have now disappeared into the past", though what these were is not explained.

The issue was discussed in more general terms in editorials in *Party Life* of March and *Kommunist* of April 1956, and what these say may be regarded as the official line. Stalin's contribution to "the struggle of our working class against capitalism" is frankly admitted. In particular his attack on the Trotskyists and the Right Deviationists is commended, since, as *Party Life* puts it, "Just imagine what would have happened if the political line of the right-wing deviation had triumphed in 1928–29. We should not have had a powerful heavy industry and collective farms . . . and the country might have fallen prey to the predatory imperialists". Yet, as *Kommunist* points out, in the 'thirties Stalin's authority gradually developed into the cult of the individual, and this he encouraged on account of elements of coarseness in his disposition and his lack of flexibility and modesty, though the article holds that he was in part to be excused, seeing that, as a result of capitalist encirclement, the country was a "besieged fort", and thus required centralized leadership. The real trouble arose in "the last period" of his life (that is, presumably after the great purge), when the cult of personality assumed "monstrous forms" and caused great harm to the cause of Socialism. Inadequate measures were taken to defend the country during the war; after its conclusion, unsound agricultural policies were introduced; and great damage was done to the development of "social scientific thought". Elsewhere, the cult of personality is condemned as a manifestation of "subjective idealism" (*q.v.*), or alternatively of bourgeois anarchism, and it is noted that it "always goes hand in hand with pedantry and dogmatism". The proper answer to it lies in a return to the principles of "collective leadership" (*q.v.*).

14

DEMOCRATIC CENTRALISM

THE term democratic centralism seems to have been current in Russian Marxist circles some time before it was used in print. It first appeared in a declaration issued at the time of the Tamerfors Conference of the Bolshevik left-wing in December 1905, when it was stated to be the "indisputable" basis of the party organization. Since the Party was working underground, the democratic element in the principle was more honoured in the breach than the observance. It was found more convenient to co-opt members to party bodies rather than elect them, and Lenin himself was always prepared to subordinate democratic procedures to the interests of the revolutionary cause. The principle was incorporated for the first time into the Party Statutes at the Sixth Congress of August 1917, but as Lenin and most of the top leaders were either under arrest or in hiding at the time, it did not arouse much interest, and only a few minutes were devoted to its discussion.[1] The formula adopted was reproduced verbatim in the Statutes as revised by the Nineteenth Congress of 1952. Democratic Centralism was stated to be the "guiding principle of the organizational structure of the party", and was defined as:

(*a*) the election of all party bodies from bottom to top;

(*b*) the periodic accountability of party bodies to their party organizations;

(*c*) strict party discipline, and the subordination of the minority to the majority;

(*d*) the decisions of the higher bodies to be unconditionally binding upon the lower ones.

The same principle was taken over by the Comintern in the "Resolution on the Role of the Communist Party", adopted by its Second Congress, and published in *Pravda* on July 30th 1920; and Art. 12 of the "Twenty-one Conditions of Admission", approved by the same Congress, laid down that "Parties belonging to the Communist International must be based on the principle of *democratic centralism*", though the stress was laid solely on the second part of the slogan, as it was pointed out that "in the present epoch of acute civil war" a Communist Party would be able to fulfil its duty only "if its organization is as centralized as possible, and if iron discipline prevails". However, the principle found its way into the final constitution of the Comintern, adopted at the Sixth Congress of September 1928, when it was defined in the same terms as those set out above.

As thus formulated, democratic centralism is susceptible of a wider or narrower interpretation. In its most rigid form it

[1] Barrington Moore, Jr., *Soviet Politics: The Dilemma of Power* (Harvard 1951), p. 67.

means that, as the expression of the Party's will, the decisions of the leading party organs must be obeyed without question as if they were military orders, and that discussion on the lower levels should be restricted to considering how best to give effect to them. According to a more moderate interpretation, there should be a broad discussion of party directives before they are issued or come into force. The lower organs have the right to submit their views to the higher organs, and may continue to canvass them until the issue is submitted to the Party Congress, whose final decision they must accept. According to a third view, which continued to find supporters in the years immediately following the revolution, every particular issue must be discussed on all levels down to the cell, and it was the duty of the Congress to carry out the wishes of the rank and file in regard to it. In Lenin's lifetime the meaning given to it oscillated between the first and second of these interpretations, though it was natural that both the conditions of clandestinity under which the Party was working before the revolution, and the time of troubles which followed it should have favoured centralism rather than democracy. Yet as long as he lived Lenin contrived to reconcile the two, and he was always impatient with those who attempted to draw a distinction between authority "from above" and "from below".

None the less the inevitable trend was towards centralization. Yet, as E. H. Carr points out, this was not peculiar to the Russian Party, or to Lenin within that Party, as in all the great countries, political parties, and particularly those of the proletarian type, were moving in the same direction, with a consequent emphasis upon the obligation of members to obey their chosen leaders. What reinforced this tendency in the Soviet Union after the revolution was the change in the situation which inevitably affected the nature of the Party. From a revolutionary organization for the overthrow of the existing order, it was transformed into the nucleus of the governmental machine; power became concentrated in the hands of a few leaders; and the Party obtained a monopoly by eliminating all others.[1]

This process was accelerated under Stalin. Party congresses met at increasingly infrequent intervals, and when convened had no policy-making functions. Their authority was early usurped by the Central Committee, whose powers were almost equally quickly sapped by the smaller and more efficient Politbureau and Secretariat until they were eventually taken over by Stalin himself. According to Khrushchev, plenary sessions of the Central Committee were no longer called in Stalin's later years. Even the Politbureau only met occasionally, and major policy issues were decided without reference to it. Under the present slogan of "collective leadership" (*q.v.*), it would seem that such issues are now submitted to the Central Committee, which is representative in so far as it is composed of persons all of whom hold key positions in the party apparatus, though its members are not appointed by any form of electoral procedure, and their responsibilitv to the Congress has long been a constitutional fiction. Indeed, what the present Soviet leaders would appear to understand by democracy is not government by genuinely representative organs, but a wider degree of consultation and discussion on all levels; and although this would represent a salutary advance upon Stalinist autocracy, it would still be far removed from the democratic practice of the West, though it may provide a stepping-stone towards it.

15

DEVIATIONISM

ACCORDING to E. H. Carr, the word deviation (*uklon*) first appeared in the party vocabulary in the resolution "On the

---

[1] *The Bolshevik Revolution*, I, pp. 32, 184.

Syndicalist and Anarchist Deviation in the Party", adopted by the Tenth Congress of March 1921, which pronounced the dissemination of the ideas of the "Workers' Opposition" to be incompatible with membership of the Russian Communist Party. Lenin explained it as follows: "A deviation is not a fully formed movement. It is something that can be corrected. People have strayed a little from the path or are beginning to stray, but it is still possible to correct it".[1] Thus deviationism was a less serious offence than "fractionalism" (*q.v.*), which implied that it had led to the formation of an organized opposition group within the Party, though in fact the disciplinary measures taken against offenders accused of either were much the same.

The dialectic assumes that of a given thesis and antithesis there can be only one possible synthesis, and it is on this that rests its claim to be a "scientific" analytical instrument. In any combination of circumstances there can be only one correct policy, and the Party, by virtue of its initiation into the dialectic, is in a position to discover what this is. Albert Camus has observed that the conception of "All" or "Nothing" is of the essence of the act of rebellion;[2] and certainly Communists, particularly if they are Russians, have tended, as Leites has pointed out, to think in terms of absolute oppositions, so that every issue is one between total victory or total annihilation, and any decision other than that actually adopted would have led to catastrophic consequences. From this it is only a step to the conclusion that those who opposed the decision wished these consequences to take place. Leites has noted that this made it psychologically difficult to maintain an attitude of opposition, since if the Party became stronger in spite of a decision which some member had opposed at the time it was

[1] *The Bolshevik Revolution*, I, p. 200 and n.
[2] *The Rebel* (1953), p. 21.

taken, this not only proved his apprehensions to have been groundless, but also awakened an uneasy feeling that had the policy he advocated been adopted the Party would have suffered.[1]

Deviationism is thus any departure from the line laid down by the Party, or from what it may later choose to represent that line as having been. Clearly it is impossible to sustain a revolutionary movement at the same pace, as there will be periods when it is necessary to press forward, and others when it is necessary to call a halt in order to consolidate the ground that has been won. It is here that the tendency towards deviationism inevitably manifests itself. The deviation may be either to the right or to the left, the former being sometimes described as "opportunism", and the latter as "sectarianism" (*q.q.v.*). The distinction between the two is that right deviationists want to go slower than the collective wisdom of the Party judges desirable, and the left deviationists to go faster. What this means in terms of policy naturally depends on the particular circumstances. At the present time the right deviationists in the Soviet Union, as far as the internal policy is concerned, would be those who want to ease up on collectivization and make more consumer goods available, and the left deviationists those who stand for intensifying collectivization and for maintaining at all costs the priority of heavy industry.

But when it is decided to brand a leader as a deviationist, it is impossible to say what charge will be brought against him, so that a right deviationist may find himself accused of being a left deviationist or vice versa, or of being both at once, as was the case with Auguste Lecœur, the Organizational Secretary of the French Communist Party. It should also be noted that the charge is often made retroactively, so that a leader who has carried out a conciliatory or an aggressive policy in obedience

[1] *A Study of Bolshevism* (1953), p. 27 fi.

to instructions, is liable to be accused of right or left deviationism should it prove unsuccessful.

16

DIALECTIC

As it has been necessary to refer upon occasions to the dialectic,
some account of what it means in the Marxist–Leninist system
may be desirable.

The philosophy of Communism is known as Dialectical
Materialism. It is materialist because it insists that the material
world alone possesses reality, and that the products of mind, for
example ideas, are simply reflexes of this material world, or,
more precisely, of the system of material production prevailing
at any given time. But it is also dialectical, which means that
change, in the sense of development or progress, is invariably
the outcome of a conflict between two opposed or contradictory forces or elements within reality as thus conceived.
These forces or elements are respectively the thesis and the
antithesis, and the result of their conflict is that they become
united in a higher synthesis which embraces what was worth
preserving in each. Such a synthesis will then become a thesis,
as it will give rise to its antithesis, and eventually to a new
synthesis. This process continues indefinitely.

The dialectic is thus the law or principle in accordance with
which change occurs either in nature or in society. Marx
borrowed the conception from Hegel, against whose philosophy his own was consciously developed. For Hegel's conception of reality was an altogether different one, as he was an
idealist, and in his system reality is identified with the Idea,
which is reason or pure thought and develops by a process of
unfolding until it arrives at complete consciousness of itself.
Hegel sought therefore to show that this development takes

59

place according to a logical pattern, and that this was dialectical because it took the form of the conflict and reconciliation of the categories which enter into the process of thinking—quantity, quality and the like—any one of which, if taken by itself, is found to involve a contradiction, and has therefore to be combined with its opposite, thus forming a synthesis which becomes the starting point of the next stage of development.

Marx rejected Hegel's identification of reality with the Idea, and identified it with the material world, of which he held that we can only obtain knowledge by observation and experiment. But he then insisted that this material world is governed by the dialectic; that is, that changes in it take place according to the same law or principle that Hegel had invoked to explain the self-development of the Idea, which means, in other words, that matter is governed by the same law or principle as mind. Thus Engels pointed out in a letter to the German Social Democratic economist Conrad Schmidt that:

"Hegel's dialectic is upside down because it is supposed to be the 'self-development of thought', of which the dialectic of facts is only a reflection, whereas really the dialectic in our heads is only the reflection of the actual development which is fulfilled in the world of nature and of human history in obedience to dialectical forms".[1]

The intrusion of this purely speculative conception into a materialist system has led to nothing but confusion, since everything that takes place in nature or in history has somehow to be shown to be the consequence of a dialectical conflict of opposites or contradictions. Observation tells us, for example, that things move. But Engels insists that this *must* be the result of a contradiction; that is, that motion in the sense of change of place can only come about if a thing is at the same time both in and

[1] November 1st 1891; *Corresp.* (ed. Torr), p. 495.

not in the same place—a conclusion to which neither science nor common sense lends support. Ever since Aristotle it has, indeed, been a commonplace of formal logic that while propositions or statements may be contradictory, things and events cannot be.[1] But the Marxist–Leninists' reply is that this only proves how defective formal logic is, and how much it needs to be supplemented by a higher dialectical logic. Yet they cannot show why material phenomena should be governed by it, and in the nature of things no scientific proof that they are can ever be forthcoming.

The application of the dialectic to the history of the development of society is equally inadmissible, and led Marx (and leads his followers to this day) to represent, often in the most arbitrary fashion, any two phenomena they choose to select as logical contradictions which are then reconciled in whatever is the desired synthesis. It was because the dialectic lent itself to this way of treating history that Marx was attracted by it. It provided him with a principle which could be used to give the course of history the direction he wished it to take, and it was for the same reason that Lenin adopted it and incorporated it into what has become the official creed. It is by virtue of it that the Party claims to be able, as the *Short History of the C.P.S.U. (b)* puts it, "to find the right orientation in any situation, to understand the inner connection of current events, to foresee their course, and to perceive not only how and in what direction they are developing, but how and in what direction they are bound to develop in the future". Thus it provides Marxism–Leninism with its *mystique*. It is the universal law by which all things whatsoever are governed, and to which the laws of the natural and social sciences alike bear witness; and it is the recognition of this that makes Marxism–Leninism the only "scientific" explanation of reality.

[1] Sidney Hook, *Reason, Social Myths and Democracy*, 1940, p. 202.

17

DICTATORSHIP OF THE PROLETARIAT

THE dictatorship of the proletariat is the term Marx employed in his *Critique of the Gotha Programme* (1875) to describe the form the State would take during the period of the "revolutionary transformation" from Capitalism into Communism. The only other occasions on which he used this particular formula, which may have been borrowed from Blanqui, were in his *Class Struggles in France* (1850) and in his letter to the German Communist, Joseph Weydemeyer, of March 5th 1852, in which he defined his own contribution to the theory of the class struggle. Neither then nor in the *Gotha Programme* did he enter into details, though it is clear that he intended the dictatorship to complete the work which the proletarian revolution had begun.

When Lenin attempted to explain in *The State and Revolution* (written in August–September 1917, but not published until February 1918) the regime that would be set up after his Party had seized power, he invoked Marx's authority for maintaining that it could only be a dictatorship of the proletariat, and insisted that the true Marxist was one who extended his acceptance of the class struggle to include it. He went on to say that although revolutions which destroyed Capitalism might lead to the establishment of various forms of government, every one of them would be in its essentials a proletarian dictatorship, which he defined as a "a State of armed workers", and later, in *The Proletarian Revolution and the Renegade Kautsky* (1920), as "power won and maintained by the violence of the proletariat against the bourgeoisie, power that is unrestricted by any laws".

Lenin's statement in the last-named pamphlet that "every one knows that the dictatorship of the proletariat is the very essence of Marx's teaching" is a little singular, seeing that in his many writings published before 1917 he had never used the formula. On the other hand, the contention of his opponent Karl Kautsky that Marx was not thinking of "a form of government but of the situation which would arise when the proletariat had seized power" does not carry conviction, as it is clear that by the dictatorship of the proletariat both Marx and Engels understood more than this, and in the Introduction the latter wrote to the 1891 German edition of *The Civil War in France* (1871), he specifically refers to the Paris Commune as an example of one. Again, in the revisionist controversy which arises in the same decade, Eduard Bernstein attacked the whole concept of the dictatorship as undemocratic, which shows that there were at least some who, like Lenin, regarded it as the form of government which the victorious proletariat would establish.

In fact, all that Lenin succeeded in setting up was the dictatorship of the Party, which is then identified, by a convenient fiction, with the proletariat—the most advanced section of the toiling masses, and the class predestined by history to assume control over the means of production—so that whatever the Party wills becomes the will of the entire community, other than that of its counter-revolutionary elements. The fact that the proletariat itself may not constitute a majority either before the revolution or after is immaterial; and to go through the forms of an election or plebiscite in order to discover what the majority wants is not only unnecessary but undesirable, since the only permissible inference from the defeat of the Party is the masses have been led astray by the forces of reaction. This is a further illustration of that verbalism which defines terms in such a way that the desired conclusion must follow from them.

In Marxist theory, the bourgeoisie is the exploiting and the proletariat the exploited class. The object of the revolution is thus to put an end to this exploitation by destroying the bourgeoisie, which was what the Bolsheviks set out to do. Hence Stalin's announcement in introducing the 1936 Constitution that "the victory of Socialism" within the Soviet Union had now been achieved carried with it the corollary that as the bourgeoisie had now been eliminated, the proletariat had ceased to exist as a class. Stalin therefore declared that "the proletariat of the U.S.S.R. has been transformed into an entirely new class, the working class of the U.S.S.R." From this it followed that the Soviet regime was no longer, strictly speaking, a dictatorship of the proletariat, and when the Party Statutes were revised at the Eighteenth Congress of March 1939, the formula was replaced by "the dictatorship of the working class". The Statutes approved by the Nineteenth Congress of 1952 merely contain an historical reference to the establishment of the dictatorship of the proletariat as a result of the October Revolution, and this is stated to have been one of the factors which has "secured the building of a socialist society". The task of the Party is to consolidate the latter, and so prepare the way for the transition into Communism.

The change was, however, purely nominal, and was made simply for the sake of ideological accuracy. The new formula applies only to the Soviet Union, and even there is not always employed, while elsewhere the older one has been retained. Thus in an article entitled "The Various Forms of Socialist Revolution", published in *Young Communist* of July 7th 1956, A. P. Kuchkin declares that, "To replace capitalist by socialist relations of production it is essential to overthrow the rule of the bourgeoisie and to establish a dictatorship of the proletariat". This insistence upon the dictatorship is significant because the Twentieth Congress had laid down that at least in certain countries, it had now become possible to "build Socialism" by parliamentary means, and this had led to the belief in certain quarters that the Communist Parties of such countries would be instructed to enter into a genuine collaboration with other "workers' parties". Yet it is repeatedly pointed out that not only is there to be no concession to bourgeois ideology, which the Socialist Parties have been accused over the years of supporting, but that the victory of Socialism can only be achieved under the leadership of the working class —that is, of the Communist Party—and will be carried out by a proletarian dictatorship. An article by G. Anatolyev, published in *International Life* of October 10th 1956, makes the position clear: "Marxism holds that the essence of the socialist revolution in the transition period under all conditions is the dictatorship of the proletariat. The parliamentary road to Socialism is impossible without the establishment of this dictatorship."

18

DOGMATISM

DOGMATISM—or Talmudism,[1] as Stalin at times called it—is defined in the *Short Philosophical Dictionary* as "the uncritical acceptance of dogma without considering the conditions of its application"; that is, the notion that Marxism–Leninism constitutes a body of fixed principles which supplies "ready-made solutions" to any problem that arises. The dictionary points out that Marx and Engels always insisted that their teaching was "not a dogma, but a guide to action", that Lenin fought

[1] The second edition of the *Large Soviet Encyclopaedia* says that the "*Talmud* is characterized by the sanctification of class inequality, slavery, the dominant position of the rabbis, national individualism, the subject position of women and the preaching of humility and submission to the toilers". It defines a *Talmudist* (figuratively) as "a pedant, dogmatist, formalist, doctrinaire".

against the dogmatic vulgarization of Marxism, and that Stalin had done the same.

Marxist–Leninist theory opposes to dogmatism "creative Marxism", which is here defined as "truly revolutionary Marxism", "a guide to revolutionary action" as "a progressive science which does not stand still but moves forward with life itself and moves life forward". It gives as an illustration that chosen, not without good reason, by Stalin in his *Concerning Marxism in Linguistics* (1950), when he attacked as "dogmatists and Talmudists" those who invoked Engels's assertion that after the socialist revolution the State would disappear—an embarrassing prediction which he had sought to explain away in his Reports to the Sixteenth, Seventeenth and Eighteenth Congresses of 1930, 1934 and 1939.

Again, an article in the *Cominform Journal* of August 4th 1950 pointed out that whereas "in the forties of the last century . . . Marx and Engels had concluded that a socialist revolution could not be victorious in a single country, and that it would be victorious only as a result of a joint blow in all or in most of the civilized countries. . . . Lenin, proceeding from Marxist theory, came to the conclusion that in the new conditions of development the socialist revolution could prove fully victorious in any given country". The article declared that these conclusions "not only contradict but exclude each other", but proceeded to condemn those "dogmatists and Talmudists" who argued that one or the other must therefore be incorrect, seeing that each was valid for its own period, the first for that of pre-monopoly Capitalism, and the second for that of monopoly Capitalism.

Now it is true that political principles have always to be applied with a certain flexibility, since they require to be adapted to changes in social conditions. Moreover, any body of doctrine, if it is not to become ossified, must contain within itself a principle of development, so that Stalin was on unassailable ground in maintaining that the Marxist–Leninist creed should not be regarded as a collection of formulæ which "will serve for every period and country, for every possible contingency". What vitiated his case was that the doctrine was never allowed to develop freely, as its application to any particular situation was determined by the fiat of an *élite*, and ultimately by himself.

Insistence upon its flexibility is in fact a device to enable Communists to escape from the untenable positions which the rigidity of their doctrine creates, and to reconcile contradictions between their theory and practice when these become so glaring as to cause embarrassment.

19

ECONOMISM

ECONOMISM was the view which came to be held in certain Russian Social Democratic circles in the closing years of the last century that proletarian activity should be restricted to the economic field, that is, to forming trade unions and organizing strikes, its more moderate exponents holding that political activity would only divide the workers, and its more extreme section that economic activity would in itself generate a revolutionary situation. From this view Lenin sharply dissented, and he attacked it in his *What is to be Done?* (1902) on the ground that trade unionism was "ideological enslavement to the bourgeoisie". His meaning was that it led to reformism— the belief that the lot of the workers could be remedied by obtaining concessions from the capitalists in the form of higher wages and the like—whereas he held that their only hope of salvation lay in bringing about a revolution that would destroy the capitalist system altogether, and that they must therefore organize themselves politically, because they could not obtain economic power until they had first secured political power.

Lenin secured the defeat of the "Economists". But the term economism is still currently used to condemn the policy of subordinating the political to the economic struggle. In a speech of November 6th 1949, Malenkov had defined the tasks of Communist Parties as the prosecution of the "peace campaign" and the securing of working-class unity "from below". The struggle for higher wages was to be indissolubly linked with the "peace campaign", which was openly political and designed to frustrate the military preparations of the Western Powers. The French Communist Party soon discovered, however, that the workers were more interested in the "fight for bread" than in the "fight for peace", and this led the leaders to emphasize the danger of economism, and to press for an extension of factory cells, which could be relied upon to support the Party's political line, as opposed to the trade union sections in the factories, to which the great majority of the workers belonged and which were primarily concerned with improving their conditions.[1] In 1951 the *Cominform Journal* adopted the same attitude, pointing out that failure to create factory cells and reliance upon trade union organization constituted economism, and instancing Italy, where many factories had no cells and only factory councils.

More recently, the Chinese Communist Party has been devoting its attention to economism, which it defines as the subordination of long-term to short-term considerations, and the placing of too much emphasis on providing the workers with comforts and amenities and too little upon increasing production. Party cadres which have promoted schemes of social welfare judged by the leaders to be premature have

[1] Auguste Lecœur and Raymond Guyot in *Humanité* of March 22nd and March 24th 1950.

therefore been severely criticized.[1] In fact economism is closely linked with "tailism" (*q.v.*), that is, failure to lead the masses, as will occur when their demands are satisfied at the expense of the national economy.

20

EQUALITARIANISM

MARX and Engels held that "equality", like such terms as "freedom" and "justice", was meaningless as long as "exploitation" existed. Thus Engels explains in *Anti-Dühring* that when the bourgeoisie raised the cry for equality in its struggle against feudalism, the proletariat joined in; but that whereas the demand of the bourgeoisie was for the abolition of class privilege, that of the proletariat, with its deeper insight, was for the abolition of classes themselves. And this, he declares, is "the real content of the proletarian demand for equality . . . and any demand which goes beyond it passes into absurdity".

In his *Critique of the Gotha Programme*, Marx took it for granted that there would be complete equality in a fully communist society in which the slogan of "From each according to his abilities to each according to his needs" would apply. But he does not tell us how such a state of things, which would require *inter alia* a complete transformation of human nature, is to be brought about, and he makes clear that he is concerned only with society as it emerges from the breakdown of the capitalist order, and that in this men will still have to be paid "according to their work"; that is, according to the services they render to the community, which are necessarily unequal. His position appears to have been that of Engels, though it is less clearly expressed.

[1] H. Arthur Steiner, "Trade Unions in Mao's China" (*Problems of Communism*) March–April 1956, pp. 29–34.

Lenin wholeheartedly endorsed Engels's thesis. In a speech of May 6th 1919 he declared that:

"Engels was a thousand times right when he wrote that any demand for equality which goes beyond the demand for the abolition of classes is a stupid and absurd prejudice. Bourgeois professors tried to use the argument about equality in order to expose us by saying that we wanted to make all men equal. . . . But owing to their ignorance, they did not know that the Socialists . . . and precisely the founders of modern scientific Socialism, Marx and Engels, said: equality is an empty phrase unless by equality is meant the abolition of classes, and in that respect we are in favour of equality. But the claim that we want to make all men equal to each other is . . . a stupid invention of the intellectuals".[1]

Yet in his *State and Revolution*, written in August 1917 to explain the type of society the revolution would set up, Lenin described the reduction of the salaries of all officials to "the level of workmen's wages" as a "simple and self-evident democratic measure", in which he followed Marx, who had commended the Paris Commune in his *Civil War in France* for introducing this practice. In the same writing he maintained, indeed, that it was an "immediate object" of the revolution that the above should apply to "technicians, managers and book-keepers, as well as *all* officials", and in fact there seemed no reason why it should not, seeing that Capitalism, in his view, had reduced business administration to the "simple operation of registration, filing and checking that . . . can easily be performed by any literate person."

This was an illusion, as he was soon to discover. Already in his *Can the Bolsheviks Retain State Power?* (October 1917) he

[1] Quoted by Stalin in his Report to the Seventeenth Congress of 1934 (*Leninism*, p. 522).

had begun to hedge, as he now pointed out that "We shall probably only gradually introduce equality of pay for all work in its full extent, leaving a higher pay for experts during the transition period". Apart from the obligation at first imposed on party members not to accept a higher salary than "workers' wages", there were two distinct problems—equality of remuneration as applied to specialists, the majority of whom were members of the bourgeoisie, and as applied to the workers as a class. As to the former, Lenin succeeded with some difficulty in persuading the Party to agree to their receiving market rates, though their employment was never regarded as more than a temporary necessity. But where the workers were concerned, equality of pay was never practised, as the nature of the work and the qualifications for performing it were taken into consideration from the first. Already by January 1919 the First All-Russian Congress of Trade Unions had decided that wages policy must be based on incentives, for example, on piece-work, and on strictly fixed norms where piece-work was inapplicable. The Congress divided all groups, whether administrative personnel or industrial workers, into twelve categories, graded according to degrees of skill, the differential being in the ratio of $1 : 1\cdot75$, which, though far removed from equality, represented, as E. H. Carr points out, an improvement upon the differential between skilled and unskilled labour before 1914.[1] In April 1919 the salaries of high party officials were fixed at 2,000 roubles, or two-thirds of the highest salary paid to the top-level technical and administrative personnel; and although this was a departure from the original principle, it was none the less a concession to that strain of idealism and asceticism which at first characterized the Bolshevik Party when party members felt called upon to set a good example.

[1] *The Bolshevik Revolution*, II, pp. 202–3.

The N.E.P. period marked a retreat from equalitarianism, and produced a situation in which wage differentials were much the same as those in capitalist countries at a similar stage of economic development.[1] None the less the tradition that equalitarianism constituted the ideal persisted during the 'twenties, until in his *"uravnilovka"* speech of June 23rd 1931 Stalin once and for all denounced it. He attributed the lack of progress in the first Five-Year Plan to "the Leftist practice of wage equalization", which meant, as he explained, that in many factories the difference between skilled and unskilled labour was practically wiped out. As usual, he insisted, though perhaps with more justification than was sometimes the case, that his policy represented no departure from the communist canon:

"Marx and Engels said that the difference between skilled and unskilled labour would exist even under Socialism, even after classes had been abolished; that only under Communism would this difference disappear; and that therefore, even under Socialism, wages must be paid according to the work performed, and not according to needs. But the equalitarians among our business executives and trade union officials do not agree, and believe that under our Soviet system the difference has already disappeared. Who is right, Marx and Engels or the equalitarians?"

In his Report to the Seventeenth Congress of January 26th 1934 he reverted to the same theme in even stronger terms, maintaining that every "real Leninist" knows that the demand for "equalization in the sphere of requirements and individual life is a piece of reactionary petty-bourgeois absurdity worthy of a sect of primitive ascetics", and this time arguing that although socialist and communist societies were to be dis-

[1] Barrington Moore, Jr., *op. cit.*, p. 184.

tinguished, "Marxism proceeds from the assumption that people's tastes and requirements are not and cannot be identical, equal in quality or in quantity, either in the period of Socialism or in the period of Communism".

Thus George Orwell's gibe that in the Soviet Union "All men are equal, but some are more equal than others" is not entirely fair, as even Lenin early abandoned equalitarianism save as an ultimate objective. Yet it is certain that neither Marx nor Engels would have thought it proper that differentials in wages and salaries, which are bound to create barriers between the various social groups, should be greater in a socialist country than in any other, as they now are in the Soviet Union, where they have come to constitute a serious problem for the rulers. Yet the process was inevitable once Stalin decided that everything was to be sacrificed to building up the internal strength of the Soviet Union as rapidly as possible; and this policy, of which "Socialism in one country" was the slogan, became imposed once it was evident that Lenin's belief that the West was ripe for revolution had no foundation, and that the Soviet Union stood alone in a world which its theory and practice was doing its utmost to render a hostile one. As therefore the rate of industrial development has alone counted, the Soviet rulers have shown little interest in guaranteeing minimum wages. They have used material incentives to the ultimate limit, and in so doing have produced a society markedly less equalitarian than any in the West.

21

FORMALISM

THE *Political Dictionary* defines formalism as "putting to the forefront the outer side of a question, the detachment of form from content"; and Art. 2 of the revised Party Statutes of 1952 lays down that "a passive and formal attitude on the part of Communists towards the decisions of the Party weakens its effectiveness, and is thus incompatible with membership". The term is principally employed in two contexts—public administration and the cultural field. In the first, it is virtually synonymous with bureaucratism, that is, with the carrying out of orders mechanically and without entering into their spirit. The dictionary cites as an example the case of a Rayon Committee in Kazakhstan. The Central Committee of the republic had passed a resolution to the effect that a type of so-called "cyclic working" was not being applied satisfactorily in the mines of a certain area. The Rayon Committee of the area thereupon issued instructions that every party organization in the various pits was to discuss the matter at its next meeting, without regard to the fact that in certain of them the new system had been introduced and was being successfully operated. The secretary of one such pit wished to put another matter on his agenda, but the Rayon Committee secretary forbade this, and insisted, against all reason, that only the question of "cyclic working" had to be discussed. The moral drawn is that such action stifles initiative, and leads to the suppression of discussion upon questions that are really important.

As applied to the cultural field, formalism is a blanket term, employed in a number of pejorative senses. It denotes the preoccupation of the artist, whether writer, painter or composer, with the formal aspect of his medium rather than with the content of his work; and it is used in this sense to denigrate experimentation in new forms; or the contention made by the so-called "Formalist" school of Russian writers, organized as a group in 1916 and finally shot down when the doctrine of "socialist realism" (*q.v.*) was promulgated in 1934, that literature is primarily an affair of words rather than of ideas, and that æsthetic criticism should concern itself with modes of expression.[1] More generally, it stands for an over-all rejection of everything comprehended in the slogan of "art for art's sake"— the view that art exists in its own right and is subject to its own laws. Such a doctrine is entirely alien to the theory of Communism in which all thought and action is invested with social significance. Art is thus ancillary to the end which Communism seeks to achieve, the building of the new society, and is justified only in so far as it promotes it.

Of all the arts, literature most often incurs official censure. In this sphere the charge of formalism will commonly mean that a novelist has devoted too much attention to plot, characterization and description, and that his work lacks the requisite inspirational quality. Similarly, he is likely to be accused of formalism if he deals with the problem of some human relationship in universal terms, and without reference to what the official view holds that it should be. The meaning of formalism in this sense can best be rendered by the German word *Ideenlosigkeit*—the absence of ideas, that is, of the ideas of the Party.

Nor are these the only traps into which he may fall. He may be accused of naturalism—the error of concentrating unduly upon the more sordid aspects of life—and of ignoring that courage and optimism which allegedly inspires the workers to transcend them. Or he may have tried to do the right thing, but if his work is so bad from the professional point of view as to be unacceptable even by party standards, he will be told that he has been guilty of schematism.

Again, the term is extended to art forms which are regarded as above the comprehension of the masses, and is thus used to condemn the more sophisticated of those of the West; and

---

[1] For the history of this school see Victor Erlich, *Russian Formalism* (The Hague, 1955) and its review in *The Times Literary Supplement* of July 28th 1955.

when Zhdanov was appointed Stalin's *arbiter elegantiarum* in the late 'forties, the prevalence of such forms was branded as a betrayal of native Soviet culture, and as kow-towing to decadent bourgeois standards.[1] The visual arts and music lend themselves particularly to criticism along these lines. At the time of the revolution, the Russian artists had not only overtaken but had surpassed the most extreme European forms of abstract art, and had indeed added to the current "isms" a number of their own. As these schools agreed in their contempt for "bourgeois" artistic standards, they represented themselves as supporters of the revolution. But in art, and in literature also, Lenin's personal tastes were frankly bourgeois and traditionalist. He disliked "modern art", and had little sympathy for the products of the *Proletkult* movement, founded at the end of 1917 under the patronage of Lunacharsky to encourage the proletariat to develop its own "revolutionary" forms. Had he lived, it is probable that he would have disapproved of the Formalists and other such groups, though he would not necessarily have reacted against them as Stalin did. None the less, their views were fundamentally incompatible with his philosophy. For if, as he maintained, there is an "objective absolute truth" to which we approximate within the limits of our knowledge, art will approach that truth only in so far as it is objective, and keeps close to "real life", which comes in the end to mean life as communist propaganda wishes it to be portrayed.

Thus Soviet artists have been severely restricted both in their choice and treatment of subjects; and apart from pictures exhibiting Lenin and Stalin on this or that historic occasion, they

[1] This gave rise at the time to the story that Zhdanov was going to issue a decreee condemning the sun because it sinks in the West, the Russian word "sink" being that used for the "kow-towing" to western culture of which these persons were accused.

have been obliged to limit themselves to the "new Soviet man" in industry and agriculture, and to depicting what are, or rather should be, his aspirations and emotions. Work must be represented as creative and beautiful, and those engaged in it must either display heroic intensity, or at least appear to be enjoying themselves.[1]

Similar considerations have applied to music, where the criterion has once again been that it should be inspirational, simple and "popular with the broad masses". Under Zhdanov's direction, the campaign for ideological orthodoxy in this field was initiated by the resolution of the Central Committee of February 10th 1948 condemning V. Muradeli's opera *The Great Friendship*, which had been produced in the previous year on the occasion of the thirtieth anniversary of the October Revolution, but which was now discovered to be "vicious and inartistic both in its music and its subject matter".[2] It did not, so the resolution complained, contain "a single melody or aria to be remembered", for such scenes as had "pretensions to melodiousness" were "suddenly broken by discordant noises wholly strange to the human ear and oppressive to the listener". Moreover, the plot, which purported to describe the struggle for the establishment of Soviet power in the North Caucasus during the years 1918–31, had contrived to convey the false impression that the Caucasian peoples at that time were hostile to Russia, whereas this had been true only of the Ingush and the Chechens, whom Stalin had later deported. The resolution went on to censure for their "formalistic perversions and anti-democratic tendencies" all the more prominent Soviet composers, including Shostakovitch (who had been in trouble in

[1] For an interesting treatment of this subject see Jacob Landy, "Soviet Painting and Socialist Realism" (*Problems of Communism*, Nos. 3–4, 1952, pp. 15–25).
[2] The text is printed in Andrey Olkovsky's *Music under the Soviets* (New York, 1955), pp. 280–5.

1935), Prokoviev and Khatchaturian. The First All-Union Congress of Soviet Composers, held in April 1948, officially endorsed the above, and published a book entitled *The Ways of Development of Soviet Music* which stated in its Conclusion that "The funadmental task of Soviet composers, basing their work on the principles of socialist realism, is to express the leading ideas of the present time in a simple, natural musical language understandable to the people, but with all the power of æsthetic influence".[1]

It is scarcely necessary to add that the Communist Parties of the satellite States hastened to adopt the same line. Thus the Polish Communist Sikorski recalled the sharp struggle against formalism which had developed at a congress of musicians held in June 1950, and declared that as a result a "new Polish music", based on folk-songs and popular with the masses, had begun to emerge in the following autumn. Similarly, the Hungarian Party leader Jozsef Revai pointed out that formalism in the sense of the "imitation of decadent western art" had flourished up to 1948, but that it was now yielding to socialist realism. He noted that the musicians had been among the slowest to come into line, but that they were now realizing that "music must be realistic, popular and melodious in order to express the feelings of the people building Socialism". Since the death of Stalin there has been a good deal less talk of formalism and its dangers. Yet it is unlikely that the last has been heard of it, and it still has its place among the errors into which any writer, artist or musician may fall, and against which the authorities reserve to themselves the right to take action.

[1] *ibid*, p. 50.

22

FRACTIONALISM

ONE inevitable result of the chaos to which the October Revolution led was that the party leadership came increasingly to take important decisions, particularly on economic matters, upon its own responsibility and without consulting the Party as a whole; and this raised the question as to how far opposition to such decisions was consistent with party discipline. Resentment within the Party crystallized during the summer and autumn of 1919 into what Lenin later nicknamed the "Workers' Opposition", whose programme demanded trade union management of industry and a more direct participation by the rank and file in the direction of policy. In January 1920 the question of the role of the unions was discussed in numerous press articles in which the leaders expressed divergent views. When the matter came up at the Tenth Congress in the following March, Lenin's platform was adopted by a large majority, but the "Workers' Opposition" was much stronger than the voting indicated, and its leaders announced that they intended to remain in the Party and exercise their right of freedom of criticism to get its decision changed.

As always, Lenin became enraged when policies which he held to be essential were challenged on theoretical grounds; and he succeeded in carrying at the Congress two resolutions, of which the first, "On the Syndicalist and Anarchist Deviation in our Party", pronounced the dissemination of the views of the Workers' Opposition to be "incompatible with membership of the Communist Party", while the second, "On Party Unity", insisted that disputed issues should be submitted for discussion to the Party as a whole, and "not to discussion by groups formed on some platform or other". This last was condemned as "fractionalism", which the resolution defined as "The appearance of groups with special platforms and with the ambition to form in some degree a unit and establish their own group discipline".[1] The Central Committee was instructed to bring about its "complete abolition"; and a secret clause—"point 7"—which was not made public until the Thirteenth Congress of 1924, empowered the Central Committee to take disciplinary action against any of its members guilty of fractional behaviour.

This decision greatly strengthened the party machine, and was a landmark in the development of the concept of the monolithic party. Hitherto, party members had been required loyally to carry out the Party's decisions, but had been free to criticize them until they had been taken. Henceforth, such criticism would be permissible provided it was not organized, in which event it became fractionalism. But although this may not have been Lenin's intention, and certainly should not have been, in view of his past record of activity of the kind, the result was to make it difficult for any party member to indulge in open criticism, seeing that if others shared his views, it would be easy to represent the group as a fraction. This was the line later adopted by Stalin to crush all opposition as contrary to party discipline.

The essence of fractionalism is thus the *organization* of opposition groups. How far the present Soviet leaders will permit such groups to form remains to be seen. But fractionalism is still officially condemned, the *Political Dictionary* defining it as "Special groups within proletarian parties with views different from the party line, and with their own group discipline which undermines party discipline".

[1] Carr, *The Bolshevik Revolution*, pp. 200–2.

23

GREAT POWER CHAUVINISM

THE *Political Dictionary* defines Great Power Chauvinism as "the national politics of the bourgeoisie of a dominating country which is exploiting and oppressing other nations"; that is, as a phenomenon peculiar to the capitalist world. Yet for many years after the revolution it was taken for granted by the Bolsheviks that Tsarist Russia has been guilty of it; and at the Twelfth Party Congress of 1923 Stalin denounced as Great Power Chauvinists the group which sought to weld the Soviet Empire into a tightly organized unitary State, and thus opposed the creation of a second chamber in which the minorities would have separate representation.[1]

Where pre-Soviet expansionist policy was concerned, the party line changed in the middle 'thirties. Tsarist conquests were now justified by the theory of the "lesser evil", which was first formulated in 1937, though it did not receive official recognition until 1951.[2] According to this, Russia had saved the territories she had annexed from falling into the hands of reactionary powers such as Turkey and Persia, or of becoming a prey to British imperialism. Nor had her role been limited to thus assisting undeveloped peoples by drawing them into "the great advanced Russian civilization", since its beneficent purpose could be discerned as far back as the French Revolution. Marx and Engels, while condemning Napoleon's imperialism, had held that its effect had been to disseminate the ideas of the revolution, which had eventually destroyed it. But Eugen Tarle, a liberal historian before 1917 who turned Stalinist in

[1] Merle Fainsod, *How Russia is Ruled* (Harvard 1954), p. 308.
[2] *Re-writing Russian History* (edited by C. E. Black), (New York, 1956), pp. 107f.

the 'thirties, discovered that the Napoleonic Empire had been a bourgeois dictatorship, from which Europe had been liberated by the Russian people; while a lesser-known historian, A. S. Nifontov, extended this thesis to the 1848 revolution, contending that the officers and men of the Russian armies, which assisted the Austrian Government to crush the Hungarians under Kossuth, had in fact sympathized with the rebels, a myth which has been used to represent the Soviet occupation forces in Hungary as continuing this liberating tradition.[1]

The object of these exercises in re-writing history has been to exhibit Russia as a progressive force, and thus to uphold such actions as would fall into the category of Great Power Chauvinism had they been undertaken by the reactionary bourgeois nations of the West. At the same time, the term is still employed when it is found necessary to condemn, in some particular instance, the policy of forcible Russification pursued by the Kremlin; and the Moscow-appointed officials of a non-Russian Soviet republic are liable to be accused of it if the measures they adopt unduly excite the resentment of the local population.

24

IMPERIALISM

THE term imperialism has largely replaced Capitalism in the Communist vocabulary. It is also used as a synonym for colonialism, which, oddly enough, is not to be found in any Russian dictionary of foreign words, and was first given currency by Krushchev and Bulganin during their Asian tour in 1955. Since then it has been the subject of numerous articles in Russian periodicals which describe conditions in territories

[1] Ruth Fischer, *Von Lenin zu Mao* (Düsseldorf-Köln, 1956), pp. 63–5.

under British administration with the usual irresponsible mendacity.

The concept of imperialism derives from Lenin's *Imperialism: The Highest Stage of Capitalism* (1916), the most revolutionary writing of this century, as communist policy has been largely based on its conclusions, and of all the Marxist–Leninist texts the most important for an understanding of the present communist world-view. Lenin's immediate object was to explain why the capitalist system still persisted in spite of its contradictions, and why the conditions of the European workers, or at least of a section of them, had greatly improved, although Marx had declared that they must inevitably worsen. He did this by asserting that there had entered into the situation a new factor which had not existed in Marx's day, and that this was imperialism, the emergence of which he dates precisely from 1898–1900.

Briefly, the essential features of imperialism are the concentration of capital, the merging of industrial and banking capital into "finance capital" and the division of the world between national and international monopolies. Lenin called this "moribund capitalism", as it represented, in his view, the last stage of the capitalist system which precedes its final collapse and the victory of the proletariat. It should be observed that imperialism thus denotes the predominance of a certain form of capital. It does not signify the direct domination over foreign lands, though such domination usually takes place. But Lenin does not seem to have regarded the actual possession of an empire as essential to it, so that, according to his theory, the United States is an imperialist Power, as communist propaganda daily represents it.

How then did imperialism come about? Because the more developed countries had reached a point at which they were producing more goods than their home markets could absorb, and were therefore driven to find markets in backward countries, which were then annexed, to which they could sell these surplus products in exchange for cheap raw materials. Thus the development of the capitalist system rendered the possession of colonies essential. But Lenin held that there were now no more of them to be had, and that a country could thus satisfy its needs only by seizing those of another. This scramble operated in accordance with the so-called Law of the Uneven Development of Capitalism; that is, success depended on the relative strength of the contending parties, which was a variable factor, since as that of one country increased, that of another declined. Hence Lenin concluded that imperialism must lead to war, as the great Powers would be forever falling out among themselves, the less fortunate being discontented with their share of the colonial market, which they would seek to extend as soon as they were strong enough to do so. This theory of the inevitability of war in the period of imperialist capitalism was modified by the Twentieth Congress, partly because it was useless for the Communists to organize world-wide peace campaigns if wars could not be prevented, and partly because the greater part of the colonial world had regained its independence during the last ten years, though without the capitalist countries collapsing as they should have done.[1] But the theory enabled Lenin to declare that the First World War was an imperialist one; that is, that it was fundamentally a struggle between the imperialist Powers for markets; and the Second World War was pronounced to be the same until Hitler attacked the Soviet Union, when its character immediately changed.

The theory led to other conclusions also. Investment abroad at higher rates of interest than were obtainable at home

[1] None the less, an article in *Young Communist* of June 1956 reaffirmed the Leninist doctrine in its most intransigent form.

increased the number of parasitic rentier class, and thus sharpened the class struggle. Yet Lenin none the less argued, not altogether consistently, that the "super-profits" obtained by exploiting backward peoples enabled the capitalists of the metropolitan countries to weaken the revolutionary zeal of the workers, particularly those in the upper strata, by bribing them with higher wages and better conditions at the expense of the new proletariat of the exploited countries.

Again, the theory provided a justification of the October Revolution. According to the Marxist analysis, the proletarian revolution should take place in the most highly industrialized country, because it would be in such a country that the contradictions inherent in capitalism would be most fully developed. The introduction of this new factor of imperialism made it possible to evade this conclusion, as industrially backward countries could now be represented as simply appendages of the metropolitan countries. Thus the revolution might well take place in one that was only partially developed, as it had done in Russia because that country was "the weakest link in the capitalist chain".[1] A rider to the above was Lenin's statement that "Socialism is possible . . . even in one country", which was to be the basis of Stalin's policy from 1924 onwards.

Thus the doctrine could be used to serve the following purposes:

(1) To provide an explanation of why Marx's Law of Increasing Misery had not been fulfilled, at least in the imperialist countries.

[1] It can be argued that Lenin's position had been foreshadowed by Marx in *The Class Struggles in France* (1850), where he says, "Violent outbreaks most naturally occur rather in the extremities of the bourgeois body than in its heart, since the possibility of adjustment is greater here than there." But he did not develop this further, and his followers had every reason to assume, on his analysis, that the revolution would take place in a highly industrialized country.

(2) To account for why the proletarian revolution had occurred in a country which did not satisfy Marx's requirements.

(3) To demonstrate that all wars between imperialist countries could be explained in economic terms.

(4) To emphasize that the best way to promote the world revolutionary struggle was to stir up the peoples of the backward countries, thus cutting the tap-roots of the prosperity of the metropolitan countries, which would then have to reduce wages and cut down social services, thus proving that reforms were no substitute for revolution, as Marx had always contended.

Lenin's doctrine illustrates the weakness of monocausal explanations of highly complex phenomena, and is open to criticism at many points. Thus the Austrian economist Joseph Schumpeter has pointed out that a State is not imperialist if it pursues a concrete interest and abandons its aggressive attitude once this has been secured. What characterizes imperialism is that it is aggression which is objectless and irrational. It first appears in history with peoples whose circumstances led them to acquire a predatory disposition and a corresponding social organization before they settled permanently, so that the urge to conquer and subdue became an atavism, persisting long after the need to do so had disappeared. Certainly it is not a reflex of the capitalist system, which engenders, particularly among the workers, an attitude of mind which is strongly anti-imperialist, so that, as Schumpeter says, "modern pacifism is unquestionably a phenomenon of the capitalist world". He adduces the example of the United States, which had no lack of opportunities, and even of excuses, for pursuing an imperialist policy which it did not in fact adopt. As for Britain, he maintains that the greater part of its colonial empire was acquired in the pre-capitalist period, the conquerors being either adventurers unable to find a foothold at home, or men who had been driven into exile. The State had little to do with the matter, and only interfered, generally with extreme reluctance, when a colony was in existence. It was indeed the Conservative Disraeli who first introduced the notion of imperialism into British politics at the general election of 1874, though it was he who had declared in 1852 that "These wretched colonies . . . are a millstone round our necks". Yet his "Imperial Federation" did not extend beyond welding the existing empire into a closer union under the Crown. Once this idea had caught the popular imagination as according with the growing wealth and power of the country, it had served its purpose, and he did not attempt to harness it to an expansionist policy, nor would he have carried the electorate with him had he done so.[1] It was not indeed until the middle 'nineties that the British Goverment, under Chamberlain, embarked upon a policy which can fairly be described as imperialist.

Again, Raymond Aron has pointed out that neither of the two World Wars were imperialist in the Leninist sense that they were due to economic rivalry, that this rivalry was the result of a struggle for colonies and that millions of men were thus sent to their deaths to open up new markets. In the twenty years before the first war the capitalist system had never been so flourishing, and the wealth of Germany had doubled. England and Germany were each other's best customers, and although there was friction, it was never remotely to the interest of the capitalists of either country to go to war on this account. The Leninist theory is based upon the myth that there existed an entity called "German (or alternatively British) capitalism", pursuing in full awareness long-range objectives, and manipulating governments to serve its econo-

[1] *Imperialism and Social Classes*, pp. 7, 16f, 24, 36, 92f.

mic interests. It is true that once such interests have been created, the banks and big business will use pressure to maintain them. But their creation has rarely been due to the pursuit of capitalist profits, but rather to the political ambition of governments, which is then camouflaged by invoking economic motives, seeing that every epoch finds its own formula for dissimulating the will to power. These motives are then accepted at their face value, and become transformed into the real causes of conflict.[1]

What therefore vitiates Lenin's theory is the false association he makes between imperialism and capitalism, and his assumption that there is a direct causal relationship between the two— a view which reflects the fundamental Marxist axiom that every phenomenon must have an economic explanation. At the same time, his theory is of value to Communists, since if imperialism can be predicated only of capitalism, it follows that colonial expansion by a country which is not capitalist cannot be imperialist.

25

INNER-PARTY DEMOCRACY

ACCORDING to the *Political Dictionary*, inner-party democracy is the consistent application of the principles of "democratic centralism" (*q.v.*), though, to be more accurate, it stands for its democratic as opposed to its dominant centralized aspect. The *Large Soviet Encyclopædia* makes its essential elements the elective character of party bodies, and their obligation periodically to report to their party organizations, and declares that it

[1] "The Leninist Myth of Imperialism" (*Partisan Review*, November-December 1951), pp. 646f. See also E. W. Winslow's most interesting study, "Marxian, Liberal and Sociological Theories of Imperialism" (*Journal of Political Economy*, December 1931).

implies a "collegial work spirit", thus connecting it with the principle of collective leadership. The Party Statutes contain numerous references to it, though it is nowhere explicitly defined. Thus the revised Statutes of 1952 declare that:

"The free and business-like discussion of questions of party policy in individual organizations or in the party as a whole is the inalienable right of every party member, and logically follows from inner-party democracy. Only on the basis of inner-party democracy is it possible to develop criticism and self-criticism (*q.v.*) and to strengthen party discipline . . .".

The sole reservation is that such discussion must be so regulated as to prevent an "insignificant minority" from imposing its will upon the majority, or forming a "fractional group" which would weaken the unity of the Party.

There remains, however, the practical problem of how inner-party democracy is to be reconciled with that highly centralized control which is held to be essential if the Party is to perform its functions. It may be illustrated by an article by G. Shitarev published in *Kommunist* of December 1953 with the title "Democratic Centralism and the Guiding Work of Party Organs". After emphasizing the paramount necessity for centralization, he observes that, "The great value of our party organizational structure is that it combines strict centralization with extensive internal party democracy". Certainly it is desirable that it should do so since, to quote our author again, "Inner-party democracy—this inalienable part of democratic centralism—stimulates the activeness of Communists, develops in each a sense of being a master of the Party, and draws them into discussion of questions of party policy and into the work of party leadership". But how far these admirable objectives are attainable under the present regime is another matter.

26

NATIONALISM AND SELF-DETERMINATION

MARX'S failure to appreciate the strength of nationalism—
the most potent emotional force of the nineteenth century—
is often cited as an example of the limitations of a system
which professes to explain history in terms of economic
factors only. Marx held that it was the task of the bourgeoisie
to bring about national unity as opposed to feudal particularism, and that as the proletariat had a common interest in this,
it should ally itself with the bourgeoisie, and then seek to
transform the bourgeois State into a proletarian one. Thus he
maintained that "the struggle of the proletariat with the bourgeoisie is at first a national struggle". He believed, however,
that bourgeois production, carried out under the banner of
free trade, was already breaking down national barriers. For
by establishing a world market, the bourgeoisie had under-
mined its own creation. Nationalism was on its way out, and
its place would be taken by that "proletarian internationalism" (*q.v.*) which was the goal of Socialism.

The question of nationalism began to engage Marx's attention after the 1848 revolutions which shattered the dynastic
principle in Eastern Europe, and led one ethnic group after
another to advance claims to independence. Neither then nor
later did he lay down any fixed principle. He tended to reject
claims which would break up large States and form small ones,
as he held that under modern industrial conditions small States
were uneconomic; and thus he supported the claims of the
Italians, but not those of the Czechs, Slovaks and other Central
European Slavic peoples, whom he regarded as too weak and
culturally backward to aspire to national self-determination.[1]

[1] Bertram D. Wolfe, *Three who made a Revolution*, p. 571.

Again, he favoured the claims of well-developed industrial countries, such as Germany, which provided a field for revolutionary activity, and those put forward by Poland, the realization of which would weaken Russia, then regarded as the stronghold of reaction. In general, he was guided by whether the success of any particular nationalist movement would strengthen the revolutionary cause.

By the turn of the century nationalism had ceased to be a problem in Western Europe. But the Turkish revolution of 1908 and the Balkan Wars of 1911–12 showed that in Eastern Europe it was still very much of a live issue, and one which had a direct bearing upon the development of Socialism in that area. When therefore Lenin moved to Cracow in 1912 he began to be seriously concerned with it. Both at the First Congress of the Russian Social Democratic Labour Party of 1898 and at the Second (London) Congress of 1903 the Party had accepted the right of minorities within the Tsarist Empire to national self-determination, with the corollary of the right of secession. This was in part the recognition of a basic democratic principle, and in part a tactical move to enlist the sympathies of the minorities; and it did not imply a desire to break up Russia into a number of small states, or any abandonment of the principle of internationalism.

Two main currents of opinion developed during these years. The first, which became particularly associated with Rosa Luxemburg, held that nationalism was anti-Marxist, and that Socialists should have nothing to do with it. The second, of which the Austrian Socialists Karl Renner and Otto Bauer were the principal exponents, differed from the Marxists in holding not only that nations were worth preserving, but also that, so far from disappearing under Socialism, nationalism would play an increasingly active role. What was necessary, therefore, was to divorce it from territory, where it might lead to trouble, and canalize it into the cultural sphere, and to this end they advocated extra-territorial autonomy.

Lenin agreed with Rosa Luxemburg's rejection of national-ism, but did not agree that it should be ignored, as he held that it was a force that could be utilized. But he was completely opposed to the Austrian School, whose views, if accepted, would render impossible the establishment of the highly cen-tralized party organization he wanted to create. As this school had gained a following in the Caucasus, he decided that Stalin (the "wonderful Georgian" as he described him in a letter to Maxim Gorky of February 1913) should make a study of the matter and write an article for *Proshveshcheniye*; and in January 1913 he sent him to Vienna, where, as he knew no German, Bukharin acted as his cicerone. The article duly appeared with the title *Marxism and the National Question*, and established Stalin's reputation as an authority, so that he was appointed Commissar of Nationalities in the first Soviet Government, formed in November 1917. Richard Pipes has pointed out, however, that it was of very indifferent quality, and that although written under Lenin's direction, it did not wholly represent the latter's views.[1]

In fact, as Pipes points out, Stalin made no attempt to meet the arguments of the Austrian School, and simply repeated the familiar Marxist *clichés*. Nationalism is a phenomenon belong-ing to the bourgeois stage of development. It is a reflection of the rise of Capitalism, and is destined to disappear with Social-ism. Hence although nations have their roots in the remote past, fully-fledged nations which satisfy his definition of possessing a common language, territory, economic life and national character, only come into existence with Capitalism, so that, as he says, "there were no nations in the pre-capitalist period". They arose because "in order to achieve complete victory for

[1] *The Formation of the Soviet Union* (Harvard 1954) pp. 37–8.

commodity production, the bourgeoisie . . . must have politic-ally united territories with a population speaking the same language". Thus the "typical State for the capitalist period is the national State", and States which diverge from this norm—that is, multi-national States—are always "States whose internal constitutions have for some reason remained abnormal or undeveloped". He gave as examples the Russian Empire and "the greater part of Asia, consisting either of colonies, or of States which are extremely dependent and oppressed as nations".

Lenin's attempt to investigate the matter more closely was interrupted by the war. But the train of thought which inspired his *Imperialism: The Highest Stage of Capitalism* (1916) led him to view the problem in a somewhat different light. For the war, he now insisted, was not one between two national blocs, one of which was progressive and the other reactionary, so that it became the duty of Socialists to assist the former against the latter. It was an imperialist war, and there was nothing to choose between the nations involved in it. Thus the conflict was a supra-national one, and nationalism was no longer, as it had been in Marx's day, a relevant factor. From this it appeared to follow, as many of Lenin's supporters hastened to point out, that the principle of national self-determination, the application of which might lead to awkward consequences, had now become obsolete and should be abandoned.

But Lenin refused to abandon it. Convinced as he was that nationalism was simply a bourgeois phenomenon, and that the demand for national independence was due solely to oppression, he declined to believe that under Socialism the Russian minorities would wish to take advantage of the right of self-determination and secede. Under Capitalism the position was quite different. For imperialism, in his view, had led to the emergence of a vast and disaffected native proletariat in the "exploited" countries, and thus the principle of self-determination must be upheld, since the promotion and support of national liberation movements was the surest way of weakening the capitalist world.

On seizing power, the Bolsheviks lost no time in applying this policy, which made the Soviet Union appear as the disinterested benefactor of oppressed peoples. On December 7th 1917 Sovnarkom issued an appeal "To the Muslim Toilers of Russia and the East", which called specifically upon Persians, Turks, Arabs and Hindus to overthrow "the imperialist robbers and enslavers"; while the "Declaration of Rights of the Toiling and Exploited Peoples" of January 1917 condemned "the barbarous policy of bourgeois civilization, which has built up the prosperity of the exploiters in a few privileged nations on the enslavement of hundreds of millions of the toiling masses in the colonies in general and in the small nations".

It need scarcely be said that this policy has not been applied to the Russian minorities, who are permitted to enjoy the rights of national self-determination and secession only on condition that they make use of neither. But, as Bukharin put it at the Eighth Party Congress of March 1919:

"If we propound the solution of the right of self-determination for the colonies, the Hottentots, the Negroes, the Indians etc., we lose nothing by it. On the contrary, we gain, for the national gain as a whole will damage foreign imperialism. . . . The most outright nationalist movement, for example that of the Hindus, is only water for our mill, since it contributes to the destruction of English imperialism".[1]

[1] Quoted by Carr, *The Bolshevik Revolution*, III, pp. 265-6.

Hence the Comintern prescribed in the "Twenty-one Conditions of Admission", approved by the Second Congress, that national liberation movements were to be assisted. Only, as Stalin pointed out, this did not mean that Communists were to "support every demand of a nation"—that is, that they were to accept an order of things which, even if constitutionally approved, was contrary to their interpretation of the interests of the proletariat or of the world revolutionary movement.

The most complete statement of communist policy towards national liberation movements is contained in the Theses on the National and Colonial Question adopted by the Sixth Comintern Congress of 1928. The force behind such movements in their initial stage will be the national bourgeoisie, whose demands the Communists must therefore support. But the Theses insist that bourgeois nationalism is powerless to throw off the imperialist yoke and secure national independence, and that this can be achieved only under the leadership of the proletariat, which must therefore assume control. This was for long the received doctrine and, as pointed out under "bourgeois nationalism" above, it is only comparatively recently that the Soviet Government has come to recognize that it is not in its interests to deny that such countries are sovereign States, seeing that they may well have their uses even if their governments are bourgeois nationalist and not proletarian.

27

NEUTRALISM

THE word "neutralism" is not to be found in any dictionary, and thus the *Oxford English Dictionary* only contains "neutral" in the sense of not taking sides, or impartiality, and such extensions as "neutrality" and "neutralization". Nor does the term belong, strictly speaking, to communist jargon, as it was coined in the West.[1] It may, however, be included here, as communist propaganda has given it a peculiar twist.

The fundamental ideas of neutralism were first developed in 1949–50 in the French journals *Combat* and *L'Observateur*, but its main platform has since become *Le Monde*.[2] According to one of its most distinguished exponents, the Catholic scholar Etienne Gilson, the difference between neutrality and neutralism is that neutrality is a situation of fact, whereas neutralism is something to be achieved. Thus it is possible to speak of the neutrality of Belgium because this is provided for under international treaties; whereas neutralism is the view that France (or Western Europe as a whole) should adopt a policy of neutrality towards the two world blocs of the United States and the Soviet Union, and which maintains that this should be an objective of French (or European) statesmanship.

When, however, this concept was first set out, the Soviet line was that which had been adopted on the establishment of the Cominform in September 1947. According to that line, a revolutionary situation now existed, and all Communist Parties must go over to the offensive. At the same time, a world-wide peace campaign was launched to provide cover for this aggressive policy. In consequence, it was not altogether easy for Communists to define their attitude towards neutralism. Under conditions of intensified class struggle there could be no place for neutrality, and indeed such an attitude is explicitly excluded by the Marxist–Leninist dialectic which polarizes every

[1] The *Large Soviet Encyclopædia* (ed. 1954) does, however, refer specifically to "neutralism" in trade unions as "an opportunist theory towards the political struggle of the proletariat, widely spread in capitalist countries by reactionary leaders", this being aimed at certain western European countries in which trade unionism has been traditionally dissociated from political alliances.

[2] See John T. Marcus, "Neutralism in France" (*Review of Politics*, July 1955).

issue and denies the possibility of intermediate solutions. As the *Large Soviet Encyclopædia* declares: "The position of neutrality within the contemporary imperialist system is, under all contions, not only *a dangerous illusion* which in no way prevents a neutral State from being drawn into war, but is in fact a *justification of aggression*, and a contributing factor to the unleashing of war". Yet in what was clearly an officially approved article, published in *Pravda* of October 3rd 1951 and broadcast by Radio Moscow, Pierre Cot declared that while there could be no neutrality in the conflict between peace and war or liberty and slavery, the practical value of neutralism for the peace campaign could not be ignored, since if any Western European country adopted it as its policy, it would abandon the Atlantic Pact, which the Soviet Union had defined as a new world-war coalition. Thus while the French Communist Party was unable to approve neutralism, it welcomed the pro-communist form given to it by such writers as J.-P. Sartre.

Yet although it is theoretically inadmissible for a country to be neutral, so that only recently the position of Switzerland was sharply attacked, this does not exclude the adoption of neutrality if the interests of the Soviet Union require it, as in the case of Austria. Indeed, in his speech to the Supreme Soviet immediately after the Geneva summit conference, Bulganin went some way to approve the neutralism of the governments of India and Burma, presumably on the ground that as these countries were not prepared to join the Soviet bloc, such a policy at least assured that they would not line up with the West. In general, however, there has been a tendency to deal less harshly with countries whose neutrality is clearly defined, and who therefore hold aloof from international politics, as opposed to those who use their neutral status to act as arbiters between the two blocs while refusing to commit themselves to either.

28

OBJECTIVISM

OBJECTIVISM, or bourgeois objectivism as it is often called, is defined in the *Short Philosophical Dictionary* as "Any explanation of the necessity and laws of the historical process which justifies and praises the capitalist system and conceals bourgeois views under a pretended 'theoretical absence of party spirit'". Thus an article "On the Soviet Encyclopædia", published in *Culture and Life* of August 20th 1947, declared that "A Soviet encyclopædia cannot be a mere collection of information presented in an impartial, neutral and politically indifferent manner. It should present all aspects of human activity and knowledge from the standpoint of a militant Marxist–Leninist world outlook".

The justification for this is to be found in Marx's teaching, according to which systems of ideas (or what he calls "ideologies") have no claim to objective truth, as they are determined by the material base of society at any given time, though some are further removed from this base than others, so that religion and philosophy are more "ideological" than law and politics. Marx made, however, one important exception, since he maintained that science, albeit influenced by the ideologies of the past, was not in itself an ideology, as its conclusions could be verified by empirical methods. Yet although even Stalin accepted this in principle, communist propaganda has frequently ignored it.

Marx argued that ideologies reflect the class struggle which exists in every non-socialist system of production, and that the prevailing ideology of any period will thus be that of whatever is the economically dominant class. The same view is held to-day. As the class struggle is now one between the bourgeoisie and the proletariat, the term bourgeois ideology is used to embrace any opinions which are contrary to the proletarian ideology of Communism, and which are therefore counter-revolutionary. For, as Lenin laid down in his *Materialism and Empirio-Criticism*, the Marxist philosophy is "a solid block of steel", and it is impossible to "eliminate even one basic assumption without abandoning objective truth, without falling into the arms of bourgeois reactionary falsehood".

Objectivism is thus the opposite of "party-mindedness" (*q.v.*), and is a serious offence. It is true that in his *Concerning Marxism in Linguistics* (1950), Stalin declared that "no science can develop or flourish without a battle of opinion, without freedom of criticism"; but this is meaningless as long as it is an article of faith that that alone is "true" which assists the policy of the Party. How far the leaders will proceed on this assumption, for example, in their dealings with individuals, will depend on what may happen to be the party line. The "cold-war" policy adopted in 1947, with its renewed insistence upon the division of the world into two camps, was accompanied by an exaltation of Russian achievements, and a corresponding depreciation of everything that was non-Russian, and this was duly reflected in the ideological sphere. Thus Aleksandrov's *History of European Philosophy* was criticized by Zhdanov in June 1947 and was eventually condemned on the ground of its allegedly objective treatment of western philosophers; and although its author was not disgraced, he was removed from his post as head of the Agitation and Propaganda Department of the Central Committee.

In May of the same year E. S. Varga's *Changes in the Economy of Capitalism as a Result of the Second World War* (1946) was also condemned, and was attacked in *Bolshevik* for having referred to the capitalist economy of the war period as "a sort of organized economy, thus ignoring its essentially anarchic character"; since, as *Pravda* of September 2nd 1950 pointed out,

"Every Marxist work on the economics of capitalist countries must be a bill of indictment". Varga's predictions as to the future of Capitalism had indeed been gloomy enough; but he had held none the less that no major crisis was likely to occur for the next ten years, which, if correct, would have made nonsense of the Zhdanovite offensive against the West, launched in September 1947 with the establishment of the Cominform. Thus a thesis, acclaimed as true when first presented because it accorded with what was then the general trend of Soviet foreign policy, was denounced as false a year later because it had ceased to do so. In 1948 it was the turn of the biologists, and a number of them were deprived of their posts for supporting Weissmann–Morganist as opposed to Michurinist genetics. Here the leaders would seem to have been led to their decision because they had become aware that if what orthodox genetics taught was correct, heredity was determined by factors which, albeit material, were beyond their power to control, thus imposing restrictions upon their power to create a new type of citizen, and consequently of society, which they were unwilling to recognize.

Communists are forever talking about "science", though they are without any comprehension of scientific method. No question is ever considered on its merits, nor indeed can it be. For once it is assumed that Marxism–Leninism is alone objectively true, it follows that whatever diverges from it must be untrue; and where the issue is one between truth and error, it is clearly impossible to be objective. That objectivity is a virtue is not, indeed, denied. What is asserted is that only Marxist–Leninists are capable of objective judgements because they alone are in possession of objective truth—an argument which moves in a circle and proves nothing.

29

OPPORTUNISM

IN current usage opportunism is the adaptation of principle to circumstances, the word being thus employed in the pejorative sense of "time-serving". In Communist terminology it has, however, a special meaning or set of meanings. The *Political Dictionary* defines it as "The subordination of the class interests of the proletariat to the interests of the bourgeoisie; a policy of agreement with the bourgeoisie which betrays the interests of the proletariat". The term was already one of familiar usage at the time of the Second (London) Congress of 1903, when the split between the Bolsheviks and the Mensheviks took place. Lenin constantly employed it, particularly in his writings during the First World War and in the immediately post-war years, when his target was the Second International and the Socialist Parties which composed it.

In all these contexts opportunism stood for that disposition of mind which rejected Marx's revolutionary teaching, with its insistence upon the total destruction of the capitalist system, in favour of concessions made by the bourgeoisie within its framework. Hence reformism was a characteristic expression of it, as was also the belief that it is possible to introduce Socialism gradually and without revolution. Thus Lenin described Fabianism as "the most perfect expression of opportunism", and its leaders as "a band of bourgeois humbugs whose aim is to demoralize the workers and influence them in a counter-revolutionary direction"; while the manifesto, drafted by Trotsky and adopted unanimously at the founding congress of the Comintern of March 1919, attacked "the opportunists who before the world war appealed to the workers to practise moderation for the sake of the gradual transition into Socialism".[1] Here opportunism stands for the alleged "betrayal" of the interests of the proletariat *as a whole*, which cannot be satisfied by anything short of revolution.

But, as Franz Borkenau has pointed out, Lenin also held a theory which precluded the use of the term in the above sense.[2] For he maintained that Socialist Parties had not evolved as organs of the genuine proletariat at all, but of a "workers' aristocracy" which the bourgeoisie had succeeded in winning over by bribing it with higher wages at the expense of the mass of the workers. This opinion he had borrowed from Engels, who had stated it in a less extreme form in a letter to Kautsky of 1882, and had quoted the passage in question in the introduction to the 1892 edition of *The Condition of the Working Class in England*.[3] In fact the wages of all classes of labour had, of course, increased over the years as Engels admitted; but the rise had naturally been most apparent where skilled labour was concerned, and by concentrating upon this, Lenin sought to rescue the Marxist theory that wages could not rise under Capitalism, and at the same time show that Socialist Parties did not represent the proletariat, and that it was therefore impossible for genuine revolutionaries to have anything to do with them.

None the less, Lenin taught in his *Left-Wing Communism* that, for tactical purposes, Communist Parties must form alliances with other left-wing parties, and under the slogans of the United Front "from above" or "from below" this became an important feature of communist practice. If such alliances succeed in strengthening a Communist Party, they are approved; but if, as more often happens, they fail to do so, the Party and its leaders, even if they have acted under the orders

[1] The *Communist International. Documents 1919–43* (ed. Jane Degras, 1956), I, p. 41.
[2] *European Communism* (1953), pp. 30–3.
[3] Carr, *The Bolshevik Revolution*, III, p. 182 and n.

of Moscow, will be accused of that form of opportunism which goes by the name of right-deviationism.

30

PARLIAMENTARIANISM

THE article on "Parliament" in the 2nd edition of the *Large Soviet Encyclopædia*, passed for publication in March 1955, defines it as "the legislative organ of the bourgeois State". The development of the revolutionary working-class movement in the nineteenth century, it is argued, compelled the bourgeoisie "somewhat to extend the parliamentary franchise"; but this has not affected the class character of parliament, as "the qualification franchise limits in every possible way the participation of the toiling masses in parliamentary elections". Thus in all bourgeois States the majority of members of parliament belong to the dominant class, and "in the U.S. parliament (Congress) there is not even one representative of the workers and toiling farmers". In the period of imperialism, which has intensified reaction, the ruling class is making every effort to subordinate the authority of parliament to that of the executive—for example, in Britain, to the Cabinet. None the less, in certain countries, such as France and Italy, the masses have secured representation, thanks to the Communist and other progressive parties.

For this attitude authority may be found in Marx's writings. He never concealed his contempt for what he called "parliamentary cretinism", as he held that, under the capitalist system, parliaments were simply the instruments by means of which the bourgeoisie maintained its domination, and that inter-party conflicts within this framework had no real significance. He approved demands for the extension of the suffrage, as this strengthened the proletariat in its struggle for power. But this in no way implied approval of parliamentary government as such, which was associated in his mind with the bourgeois State, which the revolution would destroy. Once the proletariat had seized power, there would no longer be any need for it, since the proletariat would constitute the nation, and any non-proletarian party would be, by definition, counter-revolutionary.

Lenin took the same view. Adapting a statement made by Marx in his *Class Struggles in France*, he declared in *The State and Revolution* that:

"To decide once every few years which member of the ruling class is to misrepresent the people in parliament is the real essence of bourgeois parliamentarianism, not only in parliamentary-constitutional monarchies, but also in the most democratic republics. . . . Take any parliamentary country, from America to Switzerland, from France to England . . . the actual work is done behind the scenes, and is carried on by the departments. . . . Parliament itself is given up to talk for the special purpose of fooling the 'common people' ".

In *The Proletarian Revolution and the Renegade Kautsky* the same line is adopted.

"Only a liberal can forget the historical limitations and conventional character of bourgeois parliamentarianism. Even in the most democratic States, the oppressed masses meet at every step the crying contradiction between the *formal* equality proclaimed by the 'democracy' of the capitalists, and the thousand and one *de facto* limitations and restrictions which make the proletarians *wage-slaves*".

Hence, in his *Left-wing Communism*, Lenin laid down that "Parliamentarianism is 'historically obsolete', that is to say, the *epoch* of bourgeois parliamentarianism has come to an end and the *epoch* of the proletarian dictatorship has *begun*". This last he described as "proletarian democracy" (*q.v.*).

Doubtless the primary motive for these strictures was to provide a rationalization for the undemocratic regime to which the October Revolution had inevitably led. At the same time they also illustrate the irresponsibility of the revolutionary intellectual who never troubles to enquire into the facts, seeing that at no time had Lenin made any attempt to study the parliamentary institutions of the West. Yet they duly became a part of the communist doctrine. For the Thesis on "The Communist Party and Parliamentarianism", adopted by the Second Comintern Congress of 1920, laid down that "Communism rejects parliamentarianism as the form of the future society, it rejects it as a form of the class dictatorship of the proletariat . . . its object is to destroy parliamentarianism. It follows that Communism can be concerned only with exploiting bourgeois State institutions with the object of destroying them".[1]

This doctrine was disavowed by Khrushchev in his Report to the Twentieth Congress in so far as he now admitted that "the present situation offers the working-class in a number of capitalist countries a real opportunity to unite the overwhelming majority of the people under its leadership", and that by rallying round itself the peasants, the intelligentsia and all patriotic forces it is in a position "to capture a stable majority in parliament, and transform the latter from an organ of bourgeois democracy into a genuine instrument of the people's will". "In such an event, this institution, traditional in many highly developed capitalist countries, may become an organ of genuine democracy, democracy for the working people". Yet it is impossible to see how this can be so, as it has been pointed

---

[1] *The Communist International. Documents 1919–43* (ed. Jane Degras), I, pp. 152–3.

out in many articles which have appeared since the Congress that the "working class" means the Communists, and that immediately upon obtaining power they will set up a dictatorship of the proletariat—a form of government incompatible with parliamentarianism.

None the less, some attempt has been made to rehabilitate bourgeois parliaments, which have been the object of so many attacks. Thus an article in *International Life* of March 1956, entitled "The Role of Parliaments in the Cause of Strengthening Peace", while reaffirming that parliaments are "the organs of the domination of the bourgeoisie" and "foster the illusion that the workers take part in the government of the State", none the less admits that "in a concrete situation" they "can exert a powerful influence upon foreign policy", and that "as elected bodies they cannot help taking into some account the wishes of the broad masses of the electorate". At the same time, an article in *Kommunist* of May 1956 on "Soviet Democracy and its Further Perfection" reiterates the old charge that bourgeois democracy "limits itself to the formal recognition of political rights and freedom", and complains that under it the legislature is separated from the executive, a division of functions of which Marx had strongly disapproved and had commended the Paris Commune for abolishing. The main purpose of the article, however, is to extol the virtues of Soviet democracy, where the workers fully participate in the tasks of government, of which the fact that they had "discussed the recent economic plans" is held to be a "brilliant proof". "With us", it states, "power rests exclusively with the Soviets of Deputies of the workers. All State organs are subordinated and responsible to them. The Soviets do not only legislate, but also directly carry their laws into effect." At their head is the Supreme Soviet. It alone is "empowered to pass laws", it controls the Government, and receives reports from the various ministries and takes decisions upon them. From this, and much more to the same effect, no one would infer the truth, which is that the Supreme Soviet seldom meets, and has no powers whatever.

31

PARTY LINE

THE party line, or the general line as it is sometimes called, defines the strategy and tactics by which the international communist movement is to be guided over what is usually a comparatively lengthy period. It is prescribed by Moscow, and is determined by the internal and external policy of the Soviet Union, to the exigencies of which that of all Communist Parties must be adjusted. In the inter-war years it was laid down at the congresses of the Comintern, though these were held at increasingly infrequent intervals, and from the Sixth Congress of 1928, if not earlier, it came to be that of the Russian delegation, which was adopted without discussion or criticism. The motive given for dissolving the Comintern in 1943 was that Communist Parties were now sufficiently mature to be able to stand on their own feet. Yet the line they have since been required to follow has been more than ever dictated by the Russian Communist Party, or rather by its Politbureau or Presidium.

It is a fair assumption that in arriving at the party line the top-ranking Soviet leaders use the same approach as any other body of persons with comparable responsibilities; that is, that they consider the various alternatives open to them, and adopt the one which appears the most advantageous. In theory, however, it is not determined in this manner, as it is allegedly based upon a dialectical, and thus "scientific", analysis of the "objective conditions" prevailing at the time. As Benjamin

Schwartz points out, a line contains certain constant elements. First, there is a theory which defines the particular stage which the historic process has reached, that is, whether it is bourgeois-democratic, socialist or in transition between the two; secondly, there is a theory of the alignment of the class forces at whatever this particular stage may be; and thirdly, there is an estimate of the direction of the historic process, which is generally expressed in terms of a revolutionary upsurge or decline.[1] It is maintained by Communists that this mode of analysis alone makes it possible to understand the true nature of a given situation and the measures necessary to meet it. Yet, as Leites has shown, this does not follow even from their own doctrine. For while Marxism–Leninism is determinist in so far as it asserts that the ultimate end of the historic process is predictable, it also contains an element which is indeterminist, as it is admitted that it is not possible to predict how or when this end will be realized. " 'Objective conditions' create certain 'opportunities' for the party, but whether it will succeed in utilizing them, that is, in transforming them into 'realities', cannot be foreseen".[2]

These elements of determinism and indeterminism are never clearly related in communist theory. Yet although it is obvious that the latter imposes limitations upon any precise formulation of policy, the party line is none the less represented as not simply providing an analysis of a given situation, but as also defining the steps which should be taken to deal with it; and the line, once it has been laid down, is held to be "correct" in the sense that it, and no other, is that which the "objective conditions" inevitably impose. Margaret Mead compares it to a lens. "There is only one correct reading for any given situation, and this is not seen as arrived at by finding some mid-point

[1] *Chinese Communism and the Rise of Mao* (Harvard 1951), p. 58.
[2] *op. cit.*, pp. 85, 92.

between lens readings which are too open and those which are too closed; rather all settings except the correct focus are seen as deviations from the single correct position".[1] Hence it follows that, quite apart from considerations of party discipline and unity, it must be accepted completely and without qualification.

Further, the analysis on which the line is based is a global one, seeing that it is regarded as unthinkable that it should be right for one Communist Party and wrong for another; and it is therefore applicable to them all, however divergent their local conditions. Thus the extreme left-wing policy adopted when the Cominform was set up in September 1947 was made obligatory not only for the Communist Parties of western Europe, but also for those of South-East Asia, all of which were required to go over to the offensive, as they did until the line was modified in 1950–1.

Under parliamentary democracy a policy can be reversed by a change of government, but where the one-party system prevails other methods have to be adopted. It may be decided that there has been a change in the "objective conditions" upon which an earlier line was based, as was the case, for example, when the Fifth Comintern Congress of 1924 discovered that Capitalism had achieved a "temporary stabilization", and that, as it could not therefore be destroyed by frontal attack, more moderate tactics would have to be adopted—a line reversed by the Sixth Congress of 1928 which now discovered that the stabilization period had ceased, and re-orientated communist tactics accordingly.

Normally, however, the change is made by a shift of emphasis. Thus every Communist Party has the general objective of "winning the masses", and if the line is to the left, the local leaders will promote strikes, stage demonstrations and make as

[1] *Soviet Attitudes towards Authority* (New York, 1951), p. 15.

much trouble as they can. Should these tactics prove unsuccessful and weaken the Party, the leaders have only to declare that the line has been misinterpreted by sectarian elements which have alienated the workers, and a more conciliatory approach will be adopted. Conversely, if the line has been to employ such an approach, and the results have not come up to expectation, those responsible for carrying it out will be accused of "opportunism" (*q.v.*). The commonest "get out" from a line that has proved the wrong one is to assert that it was in itself wholly correct, and that its failure was due to the organizational defects within the party. In this case the Organizational Secretary will be made the scapegoat, and will either be dismissed, as was Lecœur in France, or be transferred to another post, as was Secchia in Italy. This has the advantage of enabling a change of policy to be made, while at the same time preserving the Party's infallibility.

32

PARTY-MINDEDNESS

PARTY-MINDEDNESS ('Partiinost') was given its classical formulation by Lenin in his polemic with Peter Struve of the middle 'nineties, when he laid down that "Materialism involves party-mindedness, since it compels us in evaluating anything which takes place openly and directly to adopt the standpoint of a specific social group".[1]

Lenin applied the same principle to literature in an article of November 1905 entitled "Party Organization and Party Literature", in which he argued that articles contributed to the party press must conform absolutely to the party's doctrine, his immediate inspiration being the recent dismissal by the

[1] *The Economic Content of Populism* (1895), *Works* (3rd Russian edition), p. 276.

Central Executive of the German Social Democratic Party of six members of the editorial staff of *Vorwärts* who had apparently offended in this particular.

Party-mindedness means therefore that a Communist must judge every issue from the point of view of his own proletarian party, thus implying an absolute devotion to the Party and obedience to its directions. It is, naturally enough, the disposition that the Party seeks above all to inculcate, and it is the primary object of the prevailing system of indoctrination to instil it, and thus provide the ruling clique with trustworthy instruments. For in whatever may be his field of activity the party member must identify himself with the will of the Party, and subordinate to it his own subjective values and opinions. In discussing its application to literature and art, the *Large Soviet Encyclopædia* describes it as a "proletarian idea", and says that to assert its absence is a "bourgeois idea" and at the same time an equivocation, seeing that the refusal of the bourgeoisie to admit it is no more than "the concealed and passive expression of the adherence of bourgeois society to the party of the ruling class".

According to the same article, party-mindedness is an "inalienable condition of socialist realism" (*q.v.*), and is "organically connected with the national character of literature and art". "Its realization in practice is the expression of the interests of the toiling masses, the portrayal of the people as the maker of history, as the creator of all material and spiritual values, and as the principal hero of public events". On the other hand:

"The ideologists of the imperialist bourgeoisie, hypocritically screening themselves behind a non-class approach, are striving to use literature and art for cynical and open propaganda of the capitalist way of life, war, violence, racialism, etc. Disclaiming party-mindedness in word, they realize it in practice by defending the interests of the ruling classes in capitalist society."

The authority for this nonsense is an observation of Lenin's that "the freedom of the bourgeois artist is only a hypocritically veiled dependence on bribery".

The *Philosophical Dictionary* declares party-mindedness to be "the essential expression of the Marxist-Leninist approach to philosophical problems and to the conflict between different philosophical tendencies".[1] An illuminating example of it is provided by the dictionary itself, of which over a million and a quarter copies were circulated in Stalin's lifetime and upon which a whole generation of the intelligentsia has been moulded. The standard by which this work judged every philosopher was how far his system could be fitted into the Marxist–Leninist framework, so that Stalin was accorded sixteen columns, as against three for Aristotle and two for Plato; Lenin followed with ten columns; while Marx and Engels each received six and a half. To have been mentioned with respect by Marx or Lenin constituted, however, a title to inclusion, so that Democritus, Heraclitus and Lucretius among the ancients, and Diderot, Holbach, Condillac and La Mettrie among the moderns, owed the attention they received to such allusions. The dictionary revealed not only the inability of its authors to consider any subject objectively, but also a deliberate refusal to do so. It was re-edited in 1954, but although certain changes were made, as for example in the space allotted to Stalin, they were not such as to affect the general principle.

[1] For a discussion of a role of party-mindedness in Soviet philosophy see Gustav A. Wetter, *Der dialektische Materialismus* (Vienna, 1952).

33

PEOPLE'S DEMOCRACY

AFTER the Second World War it became necessary to fit the regimes of the new satellite States which had emerged under communist leadership in Eastern Europe into the conceptual framework of Soviet political theory; and this led to the formulation of the doctrine of "people's democracy", which is represented as the main addition made during these years to "the storehouse of Marxism–Leninism".[1]

The first attempts to deal with the problem were made in 1947 by the lawyer I. P. Trainin and the economists E. S. Varga and A. Leontiev, all eminent practitioners in their respective fields. Trainin declared the satellite regimes to represent "a special type of democracy"; Varga said that they were of a type "completely new in the history of humanity"; and Leontiev that they were "a new phase of social life" caused by the peculiar character of the present "transitional epoch of world development". These views, however, did not commend themselves to the authorities. For if people's democracy—the term early applied to designate these regimes—was a new phenomenon, the satellites might well be advancing to Socialism along their own "separate paths", and although they were then being told that they might do so, the Russians had not the least intention of permitting it, as they soon made clear. Further, it suggested that people's democracy was something outside the orbit of the Russian experience and constituted a development which the wisdom of neither Lenin nor Stalin had foreseen. Thus the above views were declared incorrect, Varga's being criticized with special severity.

[1] See H. Gordon Skilling, "People's Democracy in Soviet Theory" (*Soviet Studies*, July 1951, pp. 16–33, October 1951, pp. 131–49).

In arriving at a correct formulation, a number of obstacles had to be surmounted. First, there was the doctrine of the dictatorship of the proletariat, which Marx had pronounced to be the form of State corresponding to the transition period from Capitalism to Communism, and which Lenin had therefore proclaimed in Russia immediately after the October Revolution. In *The State and Revolution*, Lenin had laid down that just as the forms of the bourgeois State vary, though, "in the last analysis", they are all dictatorships of the bourgeoisie, so "the transition from Capitalism to Communism will certainly create a great variety and abundance of political forms, but in essence they will inevitably be only one, the *dictatorship of the proletariat*". Thus it seemed evident that the above was true of people's democracy, even if the latter did not in every respect conform to the Soviet model. Yet Trainin, Varga and Leontiev had held the term to be inapplicable to it, and indeed there were practical considerations to support this conclusion, for not only were the governments of the satellite countries at first more or less genuine parliamentary democracies, but even when they ceased to be so, it was imprudent to proclaim to the world their true nature. In 1948 a way out was found by saying that although people's democracy was not a dictatorship of the proletariat, it exercised the same functions; but the 1956 edition of the *Political Dictionary* finally admitted that "in a number of countries of Europe and Asia a dictatorship of the proletariat has been established in the form of popular democracy".

Then there was the question of the nature of the revolutions that had called people's democracy into existence. These were described as neither proletarian, socialist nor bourgeois-democratic, but as belonging to an intermediate type which was anti-fascist but not anti-capitalist, at least in its first stage. The presence of the Red Army, which had prevented the ruling class from seizing power, was in itself sufficient to distinguish them from the October Revolution; and when it was judged necessary, after the defection of Tito, to stress the dependence of the satellites upon the Soviet Union, the role which the Red Army had played was increasingly emphasized.

A further difficulty arose from the fact that even after the Communists were in the saddle it was found desirable to retain parliamentary democracy, a system of government which Marx and Lenin had agreed in denouncing, and which the latter had abolished as soon as his Party had seized power. Yet this could be overlooked, seeing that the Communists in fact introduced one-party government, and the various stooge parties the existence of which they permitted had no influence in determining policy. Thus it was possible to admit that "the political role of the toilers" was not incompatible with the maintenance of "the outer form of parliamentary democracy", while the fact that it was maintained served to differentiate people's democracy from the higher Soviet form.

Then, finally, the economy of the satellites was far removed from that of the Soviet Union, as considerable sectors of industry and agriculture were still in private hands. Here the solution was to represent these economies as at the stage through which Russia had passed during the N.E.P. period, which Stalin had declared in 1928 to be "an inevitable phase of the socialist revolution of all countries". The countries of people's democracy were thus "building Socialism" under the guidance of the Soviet Union, and one day would presumably reach the point at which Russia had arrived in 1936, when Stalin was able to announce that the "victory of Socialism" within the country had been achieved. How they will "grow into Socialism", and thus render such guidance no longer necessary, is not, however, explained. Indeed, a main purpose of the doctrine is to provide a justification for their continued subordination.

In defining people's democracy, all these matters had to be considered. To represent it as on a level with the Soviet Union was undesirable, and to stress its divergence equally so. What was needed was a formula which would exhibit it as conforming to the Soviet experience, but as immature and thus still far removed from the goal. This was provided by Dimitrov in a speech to the Bulgarian Party Congress of December 1948, and it was clearly official, as he claimed that he had had the guidance and advice of Stalin. It included the following statement: "In accordance with the Marxist–Leninist view, the Soviet regime and the people's democratic regime are two forms of one and the same power—the power of the working class, allied with the toilers in town and country, and heading this alliance. These are two forms of the dictatorship of the proletariat." [1]

With the above should be compared a statement by P. Yudin, published in *Pravda* of April 27th 1949:

"The existence of the highest form of political power of the working class—the Soviets—does not exclude other forms of State power. It has become possible to fulfil the functions of the dictatorship of the proletariat by means of regimes of people's democracy. Historical experience has proved that the dictatorship of the proletariat exists in two forms; in the form of the Soviets, and in the form of people's democracy".

As the *Large Soviet Encyclopædia* puts it in a passage passed for publication in November 1954:

"The experience of history has shown that the system of the people's democracy successfully fulfils the aims of the

[1] The text of the speech was printed in the *Cominform Journal* of January 1st 1949.

dictatorship of the proletariat, even when there exist several parties and social and political organizations, on the one indisputable condition that the only leading and directing force of all political life is the Communist Party, which does not and cannot share the leadership with anyone".

The establishment of the Chinese People's Republic in September 1949 confronted the pundits with a further problem.[1] From 1940 the Chinese Communists had operated within the framework of Mao Tse-tung's concept of "new democracy", which was very similar to that of people's democracy, at least as this was understood up to 1948, as there was the same stress upon the coalition of classes under proletarian hegemony, the same importance was attached to winning over the peasants, and there was the same insistence upon the necessity for a mixed economy. The first constitution of the People's Republic described it as a "people's democratic State", and whether or not the Chinese Communists held this to be equivalent to people's democracy, the Soviet theoreticians certainly regarded it as such, albeit of an even more primitive type than the people's democracies of Eastern Europe, as the country was only just emerging from colonialism or semi-colonialism. But at least by 1955 China was being treated as an equal, and an article in the *Cominform Journal* of January 13th 1956 described people's democracies as "truly independent States, headed by the Soviet Union and the Chinese People's Republic".

[1] See Benjamin Schwartz, "China and the Soviet Theory of People's Democracy" (*Problems of Communism*, September–October 1954, pp. 8–15).

34

PETTY-BOURGEOISIE

MARX and Engels ordinarily employ the term petty-bourgeoisie in its accepted sense; that is, for the lower middle class, the social stratum which stands midway between the capitalist middle-class and the industrial worker. In his *Class Struggles in France*, for example, Marx assigns to it "small traders, shopkeepers and handicraftsmen etc.", of whom it cannot strictly be said that they "have nothing to lose but their chains", as they possess some property but not much. Both he and Engels occasionally included in it small land-owners, and Lenin and Stalin (particularly the former) constantly asserted that the peasants as a whole belonged to this category. But what they had in mind was the mentality that peasants tended to develop, especially if they owned land, and apart from this, they regarded the two classes as distinct.

For, generally speaking, Marx and Engels understood by the petty-bourgeoisie the small traders who, they contended, were being driven down into the proletariat by the monopolist capitalists. In the *Communist Manifesto* they go so far as to distinguish a specific "petty-bourgeois Socialism", reflecting the views of this section of the community, which they condemn because, although it fully recognized the evils of the capitalist system, it saw no remedy for them save in a return to the old system of production and its property relations, or in the development of the new forces within the framework of the now obsolete relations, neither of which courses was possible, as the evolution of new productive forces cannot be arrested, and they bring with them their own appropriate system of relations.

The petty-bourgeoisie is not revolutionary, though it is capable of becoming so. For although its members suffer con-

stant oppression under Capitalism, their secret ambition as individuals is to become capitalists by rising into the ranks of the
bourgeoisie. Thus its position is ambivalent. As Lenin points
out in his *Left-Wing Communism*, it is in a "frenzy" over Capitalism. Yet it is "incapable of displaying perseverance, ability to
organize, discipline and staunchness". These defects are exhibited in its political leaders, and above all in the Social
Democrats, "the representatives of petty-bourgeois democracy", as Lenin here describes them, who agree in making
a collectivized society their goal, and then refuse to adopt the
means by which he held that it can alone be brought about and
maintained.

He applied the same strictures to his own people. In *The
Aims of the Revolution* (October 1917) he declared that "Russia
is a petty-bourgeois country. The vast majority of the population belong to this class. Its vacillations between the bourgeoisie and the proletariat are inevitable. Only when it joins
the proletariat will the victory of the cause of revolution . . .
be secured". For, as he pointed out in *Left-Wing Communism*,
"the small commodity producers" cannot be crushed out, as
the bourgeoisie has been, and yet "they encircle the proletariat
on every side with a petty-bourgeois atmosphere, which per-
meates and corrupts them, and causes constant relapses into
spinelessness, disintegration, individualism, and alternate moods
of exaltation and dejection".

Thus all Social Democrats were petty-bourgeois, and the
term was equally applied to any group which could not be
described as bourgeois, but which dissented from the Bolsheviks. In his *Foundations of Leninism* Stalin used it specifically
against the Mensheviks and Social Revolutionaries, and more
generally against non-proletarian elements, still influenced by
bourgeois ideas, which "penetrate the party, and introduce
into it a spirit of hesitancy and opportunism". Similarly, he

employed it to stigmatize any policy of which he disapproved, and those party members who ventured to support it.

35

PRACTICISM

MARX set out to construct a science of society which would have the same status as any of the natural sciences. This confronted him at the outset with what Engels described as "the fundamental problem of philosophy"; that is, whether it is possible to obtain that knowledge of the external world as will provide a firm basis for such a science. Now Marx starts as a positivist; that is, he holds that that alone is knowledge which is perceived by the senses or revealed by science, or in other words that knowledge is derived from observation and experiment. The contemplative reason in itself is incapable of providing it, and thus "metaphysics", in the sense of speculative philosophy, is condemned as valueless. This position was very similar to that of Comte and, as H. B. Acton suggests, the reason why Marx never avowed himself a positivist was doubtless at least in part due to his dislike of Comte's political and social doctrines.[1]

Marx's theory of knowledge is his most important contribution to philosophy. But it raises problems which cannot be discussed here, and we need only indicate its general trend. This was, as Marx laid down in his *Theses on Feuerbach*,[2] that the question as to whether or not it is possible to arrive at objective truth is not a theoretical, but a practical question. The contemplative reasons gives us ideas, but how far these are true in the sense that they give an accurate account of reality can be determined only by acting upon them.

[1] *The Illusion of the Epoch* (1955), p. 58.
[2] These were apparently written in March 1845. After Marx's death, Engels found them in a notebook, and printed them as an appendix to his own *Feuerbach* (1886).

Marx's theory of knowledge is based therefore upon the conception of the "unity of theory and practice", each complementing the other. This is still the received doctrine, and it is one which is continually stressed in order to show the relevance of each element to the other. For while Marxism–Leninism insists more explicitly than any other political creed upon the importance of its theoretical basis, it insists equally that its revolutionary theory is forged by practice, that is, by revolutionary activity. Theory without practice is sterile; practice without theory is meaningless. But by combining the two, it becomes possible to transform the world.

Hence practicism is the tendency of party members to conduct their day-to-day work without regard to the theory which alone gives that work its justification and significance, with the result that they lack "a clear revolutionary perspective". The *Large Soviet Encyclopædia* uses the term by extension for a narrow-minded, utilitarian and bureaucratic approach to problems, or for any solution of one which fails to take in account the overall interests of the State and Party.

36

PROLETARIAT

PROLETARIAT is derived from the Latin *proletarius*, the lowest class of Roman citizen, who contributed nothing to the State except his offspring (*proles*), and thus the word came to be employed in a derogatory sense. In the footnote which Engels contributed to the English edition of the *Communist Manifesto* of 1888 he defined it as "the class of modern wage labourer, who, having no means of production of their own, are reduced to selling their labour power in order to live". In the eighteenth century it was used for urban as opposed to rural workers, and thus in his *Contrat Social* Rousseau speaks of "the unhappy proletarian of the towns" who is transformed into a "respectable citizen" once he becomes a "labourer in the fields". But Marx and Engels restrict it to the industrial workers which the development of the capitalist system had called into existence, but exclude from it the lowest level of casual labour, which they call the *Lumpenproletariat* and treat with contempt as an unreliable revolutionary element. Nor, of course, do they admit the peasants, even those who possess no land. This is the meaning given to the term today, so that when Communists wish to refer to labour as a whole, they employ the expression "toilers" or "toiling masses".

The proletariat is held to be the only true revolutionary class, partly because all its members share the common experience of "exploitation" in the technical Marxist sense, and partly because the conditions of industrial employment concentrate workers of this type in factories, thus developing their class-consciousness, and making them easier to organize for revolutionary action, which amounts to much the same thing. Marx and Engels believed that, as a result of the Industrial Revolution, society had polarized into two hostile classes, the bourgeoisie and the proletariat, all other sections, apart from the peasantry, being anomalies destined to disappear with the capitalist system; and thus they held that the proletariat would eventually constitute a majority of the population. That it should do so was, indeed, essential to their analysis of the decline of Capitalism, and it gave to their revolutionary doctrine a superficial appearance of being democratic. It is to be observed, however, that whenever they are discussing in their correspondence any of the revolutions which they believed at this time or that to be imminent, they pay no regard to the fact that in none of the countries concerned did such a majority exist.

Indeed, as G. D. H. Cole points out, it had become evident by the late 'nineties of the last century that if the proletariat meant industrial workers only, it was most unlikely that it would ever constitute a majority, and that it was probable, on the contrary, that the future advance of Capitalism would decrease its relative size.[1] The difficulty could be got over by including in it white-collar workers and even peasants, but this was to make it less homogeneous as a class, since such elements did not possess the same revolutionary *élan*. Lenin therefore stuck to the strict Marxist interpretation, and defined the proletariat as "the class which is engaged in the production of material values in large-scale industrial enterprises". As such, it was the vanguard and most class-conscious section of the masses. Thus it became part of the communist legend that it had carried out the October Revolution, under the guidance of the Party, and in alliance with the poor (i.e. landless) peasants. For in his *Eighteenth Brumaire* (1852), Marx had declared that the interests of French peasants of this type had become identical with those of the proletariat; and in a letter to Engels of April 1856 he had referred hopefully to the possibility of "a second edition of the Peasant War" complementing a rising of the Prussian workers. But he had not developed this further, and it was left to Lenin to work out the relation between the peasantry and the proletariat, and make it a part of communist revolutionary strategy. It is fundamental to Lenin's theory that the peasants can never be more than the allies of the proletariat, which must always be the leader in the revolution, and must never share its power with any other class. For all practical purposes, however, the proletariat in this context means the Communist Party, which is proletarian by definition, though, as Borkenau has pointed out, the proletariat has always played a subordinate role in the Communist movement, and throughout Lenin's lifetime no working man ever had any real influence in the Party.[2]

[1] *History of Socialism*, III, pp. 971–2.
[2] *European Communism* (1953), pp. 26, 28.

Indeed the Russian Party was never a genuinely proletarian one. It is true that the Twelfth Party Conference of August 1922 issued regulations, repealed at the Eighteenth Congress of 1939, to discourage the entry into the Party of non-proletarian elements; but this was a measure of defence on the part of the leaders to keep it from becoming swamped with NEP-men, who were now clamouring for admission, and it in no way implied that its direction should be in proletarian hands. In the 'thirties its composition changed as a result of the emergence of the new technical intelligentsia, which had been brought into existence to implement the Five-Year Plans; and when large-scale recruiting was resumed in 1938, after the Great Purge, members of this "stratum", as it is officially designated, joined in large numbers, and were inevitably promoted to the more important posts in the hierarchy. A high percentage of the new-comers were indeed of proletarian origin, but they quickly adopted the pre-suppositions and values of the middle class as opposed to those of "workers in production". Thus the proletariat ended by losing even that privileged position it had originally enjoyed in theory.

37

PROLETARIAN DEMOCRACY

IN considering bourgeois democracy we saw that, according to Marxist–Leninist theory, the form of government which precedes the seizure of power by the proletariat and the establishment of Socialism is the bourgeois democratic State, a regime to which Lenin often refers as bourgeois parliamentary democracy because it works through the party system. Like Marx, Lenin was opposed in principle to "parliamentarianism" (q.v.), and one of his first actions on returning to Russia in April 1917 was to denounce it as no longer applicable, as he held that the revolution had now passed beyond its bourgeois democratic stage. The justification which he offers in his *Left-Wing Communism* for dissolving the Constituent Assembly in January 1918 was that although a bourgeois republic with such an Assembly was doubtless better than one without it, "a workers' and peasants' republic, a Soviet republic", such as he now claimed to have been established, was better than either, and that parliamentarianism was incompatible with it. The position is clearly stated in a circular issued on September 1st 1919 by the Executive Committee of the Comintern, which bears every mark of his inspiration. "What is the form of the proletarian dictatorship? We answer: Soviets. Can Soviet power be reconciled with parliamentarianism? No, and again, no. It is absolutely irreconcilable with parliaments as they now exist because the parliamentary machine embodies the concentrated power of the bourgeoisie". But that Communist Parties should make use of bourgeois parliaments "to further the revolutionary struggle" was quite another matter, and in his *Left-Wing Communism* Lenin insisted that it was their duty to do so.

The dictatorship of the proletariat, theoretically exercised by the Soviets, though in fact by the Party, thus constituted what Lenin described as proletarian democracy, which he contended in *The Proletarian Revolution and the Renegade Kautsky* was "a million times more democratic than the most democratic republic". This is yet another example of communist verbalism. Of course *if* the bourgeoisie is identified with capitalists, and is then defined as an exploiting class, and *if* bourgeois democracy is defined as a form of government under which all power lies in its hands and is used to promote its interests, it is obvious that such democracy will be formal only. But the validity of this conclusion depends on the premises on which it rests, and for these no attempt is made to provide evidence based upon ascertainable facts.

Similarly, Lenin's statement that under the dictatorship of the proletariat power is transferred to the workers, merely means that this is what should happen according to Marxist theory, whereas in fact the Soviets were quickly pushed into the background and the Party assumed control. His writings before the revolution constantly refer to the Paris Commune as the model of what a proletarian government should be—a single legislative and executive assembly composed of elected representatives of the people—but such references soon ceased once the revolution had taken place. None the less, he held it desirable to retain some form of popular representation, for in *The State and Revolution* he declared that "The way out of parliamentarianism is not, of course, the abolition of representative institutions and of the electoral principle, but the conversion of the representative institutions from mere 'talking shops' into working bodies"; and indeed it is possible that he continued genuinely to believe that the effect of the revolution was to "bring the masses into active participation in the work of government" long after it had become patent that it was doing nothing of the kind, nor indeed could do so in any meaningful sense without prejudicing the central control exercised by the Party.

Thus although the 1918 Constitution provided for the election of delegates to the All-Union Congress of Soviets, the function of such elections was not to ascertain the will of the people, but to provide an occasion for demonstrating its support of the regime. They enable the Party to announce to an incredulous world that, as in the case of the 1954 elections, 99·98% of all eligible voters cast their ballots, and that 99·79% voted for the candidates of the "Communist and non-party bloc" to the Council of the Union, and 99·04% for similar candidates to the Council of Nationalities.[1] That there are no

[1] Merle Fainsod, *How Russia is Ruled* (1954), p. 323.

alternative candidates for whom it is possible to vote only makes the whole proceeding the more farcical. Nor has the Supreme Soviet, when elected, any powers, since although the 1936 Constitution declares it to be the highest legislative body, the delegates do no more than listen to reports and unanimously ratify the decisions of the central party organs.

Nor is there the least indication that the present Soviet leaders have changed their views. As already noted, Khrushchev did indeed declare at the Twentieth Congress that in certain countries (clearly he had in mind France and Italy, where the Communist Parties receive considerable support from non-Communist elements at elections) it might be possible for the workers to seize power constitutionally, and then convert the bourgeois parliament into "a genuine instrument of the people's will". The impression this was intended to convey was that the Communists were now to accept the Social-Democratic method of transforming society by parliamentary means. Yet Khrushchev made it clear that whatever form the transition into Communism might take, it could be carried out only "under the political leadership of the working class, headed by its vanguard". That Communist Parties should use parliamentary means, including, of course, the suffrage, in order to seize power is no new doctrine. But once they are in power, they can scarcely continue to do so, if only because this would be opposed to the vital communist principle that "the Party is always right" and must by its very nature represent the will of the community. Thus any general demand for free elections is one that cannot be conceded, as they might well result in the Party being defeated.

38

PROLETARIAN INTERNATIONALISM

PROLETARIAN internationalism is the opposite of "bourgeois nationalism" (*q.v.*), and is defined in the *Philosophical Dictionary* as "The ideology of internationalism, of the solidarity of all workers". It is pointed out that it was first given theoretical expression in the *Communist Manifesto*, with its slogan "Workers of the world, unite". Marx taught that in every country the proletarian movement started as a struggle between the proletariat and its own national bourgeoisie. But the proletariat of all countries had common interests, and a common enemy in the international bourgeoisie. Hence the struggle must be carried over from the national to the international stage by extending the revolution from one country to another until the unity of the world proletariat had been effected.

Lenin believed that the victory of the Russian proletariat would be the signal for proletarian revolutions in the West, and that these would spread to the backward colonial areas. That the process had started in Russia was owing, he held, to the peculiar circumstances of the country, and did not entitle its people to claim any special credit. When the Comintern was set up, Moscow became the seat of its Executive Committee, but this was because there was at the time no other alternative; and although the eventual result was to assimilate the Comintern with the Russian Communist Party, this was not the original intention. In fact the deference which congresses of Communist Parties showed for many years to any suggestion made by the fraternal Russian delegate was primarily due to the immense prestige enjoyed by the Soviet Union, which had made its revolution, whereas other countries had not.

In view, however, of the close connection between the strength and stability of the Soviet Union and the prospects of world revolution, it was well-nigh inevitable that the Comintern should come to be identified with Soviet power, and that the claim to guide Communist Parties should develop into a demand to exercise absolute control over them. Thus the test of the true Communist became his willingness to defend the Soviet Union and its policies even at the expense of his own country. As Stalin explained in *The International Situation and the Defence of the U.S.S.R.* (August 1927), "An internationalist is one who, unreservedly, without hesitation, without conditions, is ready to defend the Soviet Union because it is the base of the world revolutionary movement". This was embodied in the final Statutes of the Comintern, adopted at its Sixth Congress of 1928; "In view of the fact that the Soviet Union is the only fatherland of the international proletariat . . . (the latter) must for its part facilitate the success of the work of socialist construction in the Soviet Union, and defend it against the attacks of the capitalist world by all the means in its power".

If, however, this was the duty of the proletariat as a whole, much more was it that of the Communist Parties which were its vanguard, and their subservience to the Soviet Union, or to the Russian Communist Party—which amounted to the same thing—was thus the very essence of proletarian internationalism. But this subservience did not rest solely upon their obligation to defend the socialist citadel. For it was an article of faith that the experience of the Russian Party was universally valid for all others, so that there was no problem which they could possibly encounter that had not arisen in its history, and for which it had not found the correct solution; and we have seen how careful the Soviet ideologists were to show that people's democracy did not represent a new development, but conformed to the Russian pattern. Thus the notion of "separate paths to Socialism" has been condemned as heretical, save when it was held desirable, for tactical reasons, to announce that there was no intention of following the Soviet model, as the satellite leaders were allowed to do when they were building up their parties in the period immediately after the Second World War, though as soon as they were sufficiently entrenched, the pretence was dropped.

It was to enforce proletarian internationalism in this sense that the *Short History of the C.P.S.U.* (*b*) was made prescribed reading for all Communist Parties. As an article in *Pravda* of October 1st 1948 stated, "The only true proletarian internationalists are those who base their activity on the principles of Marxism–Leninism, who take as their starting point the experience of the Soviet Union and the Russian Communist Party . . ."; while an article in the same organ of January 12th 1949 declared even more emphatically that:

> "In our time one can be a sincere revolutionary and internationalist only by unconditionally supporting the Communist Party of the Soviet Union and the Soviet Union itself, only by basing one's activities on the principles of Marxism–Leninism, and proceeding from the experience of the Russian Communist party—the leading force in the international Communist movement".

In his Report to the Twentieth Congress, Khrushchev admitted, however, that it was possible for countries to reach Socialism along "separate paths", which had indeed already been conceded in the Soviet–Yugoslav agreement of July 1955. He would seem to have had in mind capitalist countries in which strong and well-organized Socialist Parties existed. But the satellite Communist Parties, which had been the greatest sufferers, interpreted his statement to mean that they would be permitted to carry out their programmes without the Russians interfering in the name of proletarian internationalism. They have, however, been disillusioned. A *Pravda* editorial of July 16th 1956 referred to "the politically immature and over-credulous . . . who would fall for this clap-trap about National Communism" which, it was maintained, was being put about by "the enemies of the working class in the hope of splitting Communist Parties". Similarly, Bulganin, speaking in Warsaw on July 21st, declared that:

"We Marxist-Leninists consider that each country contributes something new to the historic process of building Socialism, and that it is necessary to develop socialist democracy to the utmost. But we cannot disregard the attempts to weaken the international ties of the socialist camp under the banner of so-called 'national peculiarities', attempts to sap the might of the People's Democratic State under the banner of a dubious 'extension of democracy'."

In these statements proletarian internationalism is identified with international proletarian unity, and not, as it always has been, with the claim that all Communist Parties must accept Russian direction. Yet it is clearly intended that they should do so; and an article in the August 1956 issue of *Kommunist* specifically attributes the view that Communist Parties should be independent (it is not, of course, contended that any have ventured to assert their right to be) to Khrushchev's denunciation of Stalin and his admission of many Soviet errors, which had enabled "reactionary forces" to discredit the Russian Party.

39

PROPAGANDA

THE *Oxford English Dictionary* defines propaganda as an "association or scheme for propagating a doctrine or practice", but in current usage the word has come to be associated with the apparatus which a government employs to explain and justify its policy to the outside world. The Soviet Government not only has an elaborate machinery for conducting such propaganda abroad, either directly or through communist front organizations, but also does the same at home through the press, radio, films, etc. In the Marxist–Leninist vocabulary, however, the term has an additional meaning. According to the *Political Dictionary*, it is "the intensive elucidation of the writings of Marx, Engels, Lenin and Stalin, and of the history of the Bolshevik Party and its tasks". Thus it means that theoretical indoctrination which Soviet citizens, particularly if they are party members, are held to require, and which is given by professional propagandists, using this term in the sense in which Plekhanov defined it (see p. 3 above). The posesssion of a knowledge of Marxism–Leninism is regarded as essential, as Lenin laid down that a revolutionary movement can only be carried out "by a party guided by the most advanced theory".

Hence Stalin declared at the outset of his *Foundations of Leninism*—the writing in which he first sought to establish his credentials as the theoretician of the Party—that "the attempt of practical workers to brush theory aside runs counter to the whole spirit of Leninism, and is fraught with serious danger to the cause"; and in his Reports to the various party Congresses, and on other occasions, the shortcomings of the Party were attributed to a lack of understanding of Marxist–Leninist principles. There exists therefore in the Soviet Union an immense apparatus for giving instruction in them both to party and non-party members; and the same is true of the satellite States, where the party leaders continually stress the importance of indoctrination, and explain the measures that are being taken to supply it. The form it takes ranges from groups which meet for a few hours a week over a given period to study some prescribed book, such as the *Short History of the C.P.S.U.* (*b*), to high-level establishments which give full-time courses lasting for anything up to three years, or even longer.

The importance attached to indoctrination may be attributed in part to the peculiar nature of the political concepts of Marxism–Leninism, which are far from self-evident, though they possess an underlying consistency. Having regard to the circumstances under which the October Revolution was carried out, it is easy to see how there arose the doctrine that the Party is infallible, that its will represents that of the masses, and that it is therefore the duty of everyone to submit to it. Yet this is not a view at which the ordinary man would have been likely to arrive through his untutored reason, for if left to himself he might well have concluded that the will of the masses could be more readily ascertained by providing some appropriate machinery for discovering what it was. No elaborate system of political indoctrination is required to persuade the citizen of the West that general elections, plebiscites and the like do provide a rough and ready means of determining what the majority of the community want, whereas it will certainly be needed to explain why this is unnecessary.

At the same time, its importance is also in part attributable to the notion to which many Communists genuinely subscribe, though perhaps less fervently today, that Marxism–Leninism is the only "scientific" world view, so that, as an article in *Pravda* of December 27th 1948 puts it, a "deep mastery of its methodology is the decisive condition for successful scientific, educational and practical activity". As Aleksandrov declared in an address of November 2nd 1946, Soviet society, which is based on Marxism–Leninism, is "an immeasurably higher social order than all previous and contemporary forms of social life known to us". Only, as he pointed out, this society does not develop "by virtue of elemental laws"—for this would be the heresy of "spontaneity" (*q.v.*)—but as a result of the "conscious effort" of those who are striving to create it, and particularly that of the leading workers of the Party and State.

The object of indoctrination is thus to develop the attitude of mind which will encourage this effort, which is, briefly, an absolute devotion to communist principles and an implacable hostility to all others. That it often fails to develop this attitude is, of course, ascribed to the shortcomings of the propagandists —a constant target of criticism—and never to the principles themselves, which, as an article in *Young Communist* of January 1956 declares, "arm the party and the people with a knowledge of the objective laws of social development, and teach the art of understanding the internal connection between events and of seeing the forward perspectives of our movement". For if the Party is to carry out its role as the leader, its members must "master" the principles for which they stand. Only not all of them will require the same degree of "mastery", as this will depend on their level of intelligence and the work they are called upon to perform. As for the "broad masses", they will receive the Party's message through "agitation" (*q.v.*).

40

PURGES [1]

AT all times in history rulers who are absolute, or who desire to become so, have sought to remove actual or potential enemies, and here Hitler and Mussolini simply conformed to type. In the Soviet Union, however, and in communist-controlled countries, this process is carried much further, and the term "purge" has been coined to describe it. It is used for three types of punitive operation, which are distinct, though upon

[1] For the most recent and complete treatment of the subject see Zbigniew K. Brzezinski, *The Permanent Purge* (Harvard 1956).

occasion they may merge with one another. First, there is general action taken within the Soviet Union to eradicate elements in the population at large which are defined as "counter-revolutionary"; though persons charged under the notorious Art. 58 of the Penal Code need not in fact have committed any specific offence, as it is sufficient that they should be regarded, on account of their social background or for any other reason, as potential offenders. The elimination of such elements does not necessarily involve their physical liquidation, though it is likely to do so during a revolution, or if the operation is allowed to get out of control, as it did in the Great Purge of 1936–8, when untold thousands of perfectly innocent people perished. Normally, however, it has been judged sufficient to send persons in this category to such camps as Vorkuta, where they will be effectively isolated from the mass of the population for the rest of their lives.

Secondly, there are the recurrent purges which take place within the Party itself, and particularly among its officials, for which provision was made as early as 1920 in the "Twenty-one Conditions of Admission to the Comintern". But in addition to the elimination of persons holding responsible party offices who are found to be deviationists, any considerable shift of power in the top leadership will be followed by the dismissal of those who owed their position to, or were supporters of, leaders who have now passed under a cloud. Similarly any marked change in the party line invariably leads to the discharge of officials closely associated with the policy which has been condemned, though their only offence may have been to have obeyed orders.

Again, the leaders may decide upon a review of the entire party membership. As the "vanguard" of the proletariat, the Party is in theory an *élite*. But from time to time tactical considerations may make it desirable to build it up into a mass party, until at last a point is reached when it has to be sifted if it is to continue to possess the requisite ideological purity and revolutionary zeal. Recent examples of purges of this kind are those which have taken place in the satellite countries. In the years immediately following the war, the Communists gained control, and large numbers of persons hastened to climb on to their band-waggon from more or less interested motives. Hence the Parties became swollen with "unreliable elements", and the leaders eventually required all members to hand in their cards, which were not returned to them until they had submitted to such an enquiry as would check their antecedents and determine their loyalty.

Thirdly, there are the purges which the dominant group among the top-ranking leaders carry out in the course of their struggle for power in order to eliminate rivals. Classical examples are Stalin's settlement of accounts with the "left opposition" (Trotsky, Kamenev and Zinoviev) in 1926-7, and with the "right opposition" (Bukharin, Tomsky and Rykov) in 1929-30—a process completed in the Great Purge, when it caused such horrifying excesses that Stalin was obliged to give the Eighteenth Congress of 1939 an assurance that it would not be repeated. The wholesale slaughter of these years must be attributed in part to Stalin's doubtless abnormal mental condition. Yet that condition is itself the product of the isolation from which autocratic leaders or groups inevitably suffer, and which, by cutting them off from reliable sources of information, breeds fear and suspicion, and thus leads them to resort to terror to suppress non-existent plots and conspiracies.

In his famous speech of February 25th 1956 Khrushchev frankly admitted that Stalin's ruthlessness had accounted for the execution or disgrace of countless inoffensive persons. But although he condemned the severity exercised against the ringleaders in the purges of the 'twenties, he held the purges themselves to be fully justified; while throughout he concerned himself only with the treatment of party members, leaving it to be understood that any measures could be taken against those who did not belong to it—as, for example, the kulaks. Nor, again, had he a word to say about the system which had enabled Stalin to behave as he had done.

In fact, the purge is an essential concomitant of communist rule by reason of the nature of the Party and the objectives for which it stands. Lenin's main contribution to the "science" which couples his name with that of Marx was his concept of the Party which he early formed and never abandoned. It was that of a "narrow party" of dedicated revolutionaries, prepared to accept an iron discipline imposed by the centre. The strains and tensions experienced after the revolution led him to insist more strongly than ever upon this; and the resolution of the Tenth Congress of April 1921 condemning the formation of opposition groups as "fractionalism" (*q.v.*) marked the beginning of the concept of the monolithic party, whose members must present a united front upon all questions, and from which every dissentient element must therefore be excluded.

This conception was reinforced by an ideology which reflects the crude and extremist antimonies of communist thinking. Marxist Socialism is the only "scientific" world view, and can alone regenerate humanity. To the party leaders belongs the right to interpret it, and with that right the power also, seeing that they alone fully comprehend the mysteries of the dialectic which reveal the true nature of the historical process. Hence every decision the Party makes is the right one in the sense that it prescribes the particular course of action which will, in the given circumstances, strengthen it, and thus assist the revolutionary cause, whereas any other decision would have had the contrary effect. On these premisses, any opposition to the will of the Party can be represented as a betrayal of the revolutionary cause.

Then there are the objectives for which the Party stands. Absolute rulers are normally averse to change, and desire only to maintain the existing order. But Communism is dedicated to the future—to the creation out of imperfect human material of a new man and a new society fashioned according to its own model. Yet it is impossible to maintain any revolution at the same tempo, since at times the pace has to be slackened, if only to enable the Party to consolidate the ground won. Further, as the country settles down, the promotion of large-scale industry and agriculture, albeit undertaken under the slogan of "building Socialism", tends to become an end in itself, and the careers of party members on the highest level become bound up with the success of this or that project. Thus is it certain that differences of opinion will arise between those who feel that the time has come to stay the revolution, at least temporarily, and those who hold that it must be pressed forward and larger and more ambitious schemes be continually undertaken. The ultimate decision rests with the top leadership, and the issue may well take such a form as to lead to a purge of its members. Among party officials it is always liable to do so, as they may at any time find themselves going faster or slower than is judged desirable, and so be accused of one form of deviationism or the other.

As long as Communist Parties exist, there are thus certain to be purges. They constitute the only way in which it is possible, under the one-party system, to deal with a recalcitrant element in the leadership which is not permitted to organize its opposition to the official line. The process need not necessarily involve physical liquidation, but it is likely to be attended by unpleasant consequences to the victims, if only because it will clearly be to the advantage of the leadership to represent to the public that the opposition has been of such a nature as to render those responsible for it "enemies of the people", in which event some form of disciplinary action more stringent than mere exclusion from the Party will be called for.

41

REFORMISM

REFORMISM is the central issue which divides Communists from Socialists, and particularly from the latter's right-wing. Marx first defined it in his *Eighteenth Brumaire* (1852):

> "The peculiar character of Social Democracy is epitomized in the fact that democratic-republican institutions are demanded as a means, not of doing away with two extremes, capital and wage labour, but of weakening their antagonism and transforming it into harmony. However different the means proposed for the attainment of this end may be, however much it may be trimmed with more or less revolutionary notions, the content remains the same".

In other words, reformism was the view, widely held at the time when Marx was writing by the various continental left-wing groups other than the Blanquists, that the evils of the capitalist system could be exorcised by reforms, whereas he held that this was impossible, and that the whole system must be swept away by revolutionary action. In the second half of the nineteenth century Marx's view came increasingly to be accepted, and was incorporated by the more important Social Democratic parties into their official programmes in one form or another.

But towards the close of the century the attitude of these parties underwent a change, and this was most marked in the German Party, which was by far the largest and best organized of them, and had adopted at the Erfurt Congress of 1891 a specifically Marxist programme. The power and wealth of Germany were increasing, the industrial workers were better off than they had ever been, and the Government was creating and extending social services. Under such circumstances, the destruction of the capitalist system, and the bourgeois State which upheld it, appeared utopian, and the leaders, as practical men, came increasingly to use their growing political power to secure concrete benefits for the workers. Thus a contradiction arose between their reformist policy and their revolutionary theory. As John Plamenatz puts it, "they practised what they could not preach, and preached what they dared not practice".[1]

At the turn of the century this contradiction was brought into the open by Bernstein, who had lived for many years in London, and had come under the influence of the Fabians. He now advocated a reconsideration of Marxism, insisting that its major predictions had been proved incorrect and that this should be frankly acknowledged. His views became known as revisionism, which is the theory of reformism, as the latter means the adopting of policies which can be justified only if Marxism has been so "revised" as to eliminate the revolutionary element which is an essential part of it. He was duly condemned as a heretic, but the social democratic parties of the Second International continued to practise reformism as before, and the contradiction was not resolved until Lenin set up the Third International (Comintern) in March 1920, and split the labour movement in one country after another by forcing parties to choose between reformism and Marxism of the authentic revolutionary type with its inevitable implications.

In the First World War Lenin raised the issue in his polemics against the Second International; and in the great controversy which arose with the western social democratic

[1] "Deviations from Marxism" (*Political Quarterly*, Jan.–March 1950, p. 42).

leaders after the October Revolution, reformism came to be used to denote the whole ideological complex which divided Communists from Socialists, and prevented the two parties from joining forces to achieve that classless society which was their common objective. The controversy revealed Lenin's complete lack of understanding of the West, which was not revolutionary in spite of the lip-service paid by Social Democratic parties to Marxist revolutionary principles.

Yet Lenin could appeal to Marx's teaching in support of his rejection of "reformism", or "opportunism" (*q.q.v.*), seeing that the two were so closely associated in his mind that what he has to say about the one applies equally to the other. In his *Controversial Questions* (1913) he maintains that "reformism means that people confine themselves to agitation for changes which do not require the removal of the main foundations of the old ruling class, changes that are *compatible* with the *preservation* of these foundations". Again, in his *Can the Bolsheviks Retain State Power?* (October 1917) he declares that "it simply means concessions by the ruling class and not its overthrow; it means that concessions are made by the ruling class, but that the power remains in its hands". Thus Art. 7 of the "Twenty-one Conditions of Admission" to the Comintern, approved at the Second Congress of 1920, laid down that, "Parties which wish to join the Communist International are obliged to recognize the necessity for a complete and absolute break with reformism. . . . Without that, no consistent communist policy is possible". Stalin upheld the same doctrine. For both, reformists are persons who, despite their left-wing sympathies, in fact become allies of the bourgeoisie because they refuse to recognize that the destruction of the capitalist system necessarily implies the establishment of a regime of the Soviet type, and thus the adoption of the measures required to establish it.

In view of what reformism stands for, expositions of

communist ideology naturally devote considerable attention to it. The *Political Dictionary* defines it as:

"The opportunist tendency in the international working-class movement which strives for co-operation with the bourgeoisie, and makes the struggle of the working-class a struggle for reforms only which does not touch the bases of capitalist society. Calling themselves Socialist, reformists propagate the idea that Socialism can be attained along the path of bourgeois democracy, gradually, by peaceful means, and without revolution. They reject the revolutionary class struggle of the workers, and deny the necessity for the establishment of a dictatorship of the proletariat, thereby helping the capitalists to maintain their domination".

The article asserts, however, that "the broad masses are becoming increasingly convinced that reformism means the stifling of their interests in favour of those of the bourgeoisie".

The *Philosophical Dictionary* gives a somewhat sharper definition, according to which reformism is:

"A tendency in the workers' movement which is hostile to revolutionary Marxism and to the interests of the proletariat, which substitutes for class warfare against capitalism, the struggle for the dictatorship of the proletariat, and the victory of Socialist petty reforms which do not touch the basis of exploitation in the bourgeois system".

It should, however, be noted that the ruling of the Twentieth Congress that it may be possible in certain countries to effect the transition from Capitalism to Socialism by parliamentary means does not involve, as is repeatedly pointed out, any concession to reformism. Thus G. Anatolyev, writing in *International Life* of October 1956, declares that the "transition demands a ceaseless fight against opportunism which, in preaching the gradual transformation through petty reforms and parliamentary resolutions, rejects the necessity for the capture of power by the working class". "As for reformers", he tells us, "the whole of their parliamentary activity boils down . . . to making use of parliament in order to carry out reforms which are acceptable to the bourgeoisie. Such activities merely strengthen reaction, and do substantial damage to the workers' movement".

42

REVOLUTIONARY VIGILANCE

THE necessity for vigilance, or revolutionary vigilance as it is generally called, is continually stressed in communist propaganda. As good a formulation as any of the reason for it is contained in a circular letter issued by the Central Committee on the occasion of the murder of the Leningrad party chief, S. M. Kirov, in 1934, and quoted in Chapter 11, Section 3 of the *Short History of the C.P.S.U. (b)*:

"We must put an end to the opportunist complacency engendered by the erroneous assumption that as we grow stronger the enemy will become tamer and more inoffensive. This assumption is an utter fallacy. It is a recrudescence of the Right deviation, which assured all and sundry that our enemies would little by little creep into Socialism and in the end become real Socialists. The Bolsheviks have no business to rest on their laurels: they have no business to sleep at their posts. What we need is not complacency, but vigilance, real Bolshevik revolutionary vigilance. It should be remembered that the more hopeless the position of the enemies, the more eagerly will they clutch at 'extreme measures' as the only recourse of the doomed in their struggle against the Soviet power. We must remember this, and be vigilant".

Revolutionary vigilance is thus related to a number of Marxist–Leninist concepts. First, that the Soviet State and any others modelled upon it are surrounded by enemies who will use every means to destroy them, e.g., by employing spies and saboteurs, and by using bourgeois ideology to suborn individuals (see "capitalist encirclement"). Secondly, that the class struggle becomes intensified in the transition period into Socialism, because the doomed capitalist world, will intensify its resistance, so that it will be responsible for the eventual revolution and not the proletariat, which is simply fulfilling its historic mission. Thirdly, that in defending its class interests, the bourgeoisie is only doing what is to be expected, and the real enemies of the revolution are the Socialists, since it is their alleged alliance with the bourgeoisie that is keeping the capitalist system alive. Thus the sharpening of the class struggle is invariably stressed when the party line moves to the left, as this carries with it the corollary that the struggle against the Socialists must be intensified; while, conversely, it is played down when the line shifts to the right, as it did at the Twentieth Congress, which insisted that it was now the duty of Communist Parties to form Popular Fronts with other left-wing political groups.

But whoever is the class enemy, and he may well be found in the ranks of the Party itself, it is the duty of every Communist Party and its members to recognize and destroy him. As usual, the C.P.S.U. sets an example in this regard, and thus an article in the *Cominform Journal* of November 23 1951 pointed out that it was owing to its revolutionary vigilance that "the aggressive designs of the Fascist–Tito gang were exposed". An article in the same periodical of February 27th 1953 cited "the exposure of the group of doctor-killers, agents of the American and British imperialists", as a further illustration of this devotion to duty.

The belief that the capitalist world is forever seeking to corrupt Communists in order to carry out its designs makes it incumbent upon every Party to exercise the utmost vigilance in the conduct of its affairs; and one lapse from this, to which reference is constantly made, is the appointment of "cadres" (*q.v.*) without sufficient enquiry into their antecedents, with the result that politically unreliable persons are placed in positions where they can act as "betrayers of the people". The same emphasis upon revolutionary vigilance is reflected in the Penal Codes of communist countries, according to which the disclosure of any item of political or economic information which has not been officially released becomes a criminal offence.

43

SECTARIANISM

THE *Political Dictionary* lays down that "By sectarianism is meant separation from the broad mass of the workers, adherence to narrow party groups, and refusal under the pretext of purity of principle to participate in the trade unions and other mass organizations". All the arguments against it are to be found in that manual of Communist *raison d'état*, *Left-Wing Communism* (1920), in which Lenin insisted that if Communism was to capture the masses, party members must be prepared to work in left-wing political and other movements with a view to wresting control of them from their socialist opponents, and that it was the mark of the good revolutionary that he should be willing to do this.

Yet whenever the party line shifts to the right, which means that Communists are required to collaborate with non-communist elements, there will always be trouble with the extremists who do not see that such collaboration is tactical only, and regard it as a betrayal of principle. The classical example of this was the reversal by the Seventh Comintern Congress of 1935 of the extreme left-wing line adopted by the Sixth Congress of 1928. Communist Parties were now told to lay off revolutionary action altogether, form Popular Fronts with anti-fascist parties, and even participate in bourgeois governments. This decision was clearly inspired by Moscow's alarm at the growing power of Germany which made it impolitic to weaken countries which, albeit capitalist, were also anti-fascist; but it was one likely to be resented by those Communists whose whole lives had been dedicated to revolution and were too old to change their ways; and as Stalin was taking no chances, the great majority of them were summoned to Moscow and liquidated.

Any party member is liable, however, to be accused of sectarianism if he goes further to the left than his leaders judge desirable, so that sectarianism is virtually identical with left deviationism. An illustration of minor importance will suffice. In 1950–2 western Communist Parties were enjoined to concentrate upon the "Peace Campaign" and upon Stalin's proposed "Peace Pact", and to create a broadly-based movement in support of these objectives. In November 1952 Roger Garaudy, the head of the French communist-controlled "Union de la Jeunesse Républicaine Française", wanted this movement to return to its pre-war title of the "Jeunesse Communiste", and was accused of sectarianism by the Organizational Secretary, Auguste Lecœur, on the ground that he was committing an "erreur monumentale" in choosing that moment to convert what purported to be an independent youth movement into one that was avowedly Communist. It is then in these "go-slow" periods that articles on the danger of sectarianism will appear in the party press, and the failure of communist workers to induce socialist workers to combine with them for common action is invariably attributed to it.

44

SOCIAL CHAUVINISM

SOCIAL CHAUVINSIM is a term coined by Lenin in his polemical writings of the First World War. It is defined in his *Collapse of the Second International* (1915) as "The recognition of the idea of the defence of the fatherland in the present imperialist war, the justification of an alliance between the Socialists and the bourgeoisie and the governments of 'their own' countries". In *The Tasks of the Proletariat in our Revolution* (1917), the social chauvinists are the socialist leaders who were supporting their bourgeois governments in prosecuting the war as one of national defence, whereas Lenin's thesis was that all modern wars are imperialist wars fought on behalf of bourgeois interests, and that, as internationalists, it was the duty of the Socialists to unite and convert them into "revolutionary wars" for the destruction of capitalism. In support of this view he appealed with some force to the resolutions adopted in identical terms by the Second International at its congresses of Stuttgart (1907) and Basle (1912), which contained the statement, for which he and Rosa Luxemburg had in fact been responsible, that, in the event of war, it was the duty of the proletariat "with all their powers to utilize the economic and political crisis created by it to rouse the masses and thereby hasten the downfall of capitalist-class rule".

The term is thus applicable to Socialist Parties which support their governments when their countries are attacked. In so doing, they are assumed to be representing an insignificant section of labour, which is seeking to defend its privileged position at the expense of the interests of the working-class as a whole. As Lenin declared in *The Collapse of the Second International*, "It is perfectly clear that the principal political and ideological content of social chauvinism fully coincides with the principles of opportunism. It is *one and the same tendency*".

45

SOCIAL-DEMOCRATISM

Up to 1914 Lenin had regarded himself as a Social Democrat, but, as we have seen, he joined issue during the war with the social democratic parties, and with the Second International to which they were affiliated, for supporting their national governments, instead of converting the war into a revolutionary war for the destruction of capitalism. After the October Revolution the rift widened, because the social-democratic leaders, on whose support he had counted, hastened to dissociate themselves from the regime he had set up. None the less, the present division between Communists and Social Democrats did not come into existence until Lenin founded the Comintern in March 1919, and confronted the social-democratic parties with the choice of either remaining affiliated to the Second International, or breaking with it and affiliating to the Communist International. In one country after another an extremist element chose the second of these alternatives and formed specifically communist parties. The split caused great bitterness on both sides, which communist propaganda did its utmost to inflame.

The "Theses on the World Situation", drafted by Trotsky and Varga and adopted by the Third Comintern Congress of 1921, declare that:

"The difference (between the Communists and the Social Democrats) is that the Social Democrats obstruct real revolutionary development by doing all they can, whether in the government or in opposition, to help re-establish the stability of the bourgeois State, while the Communists take advantage of every opportunity and of every means to overthrow or destroy the bourgeois State".[1]

Reduced to its simplest terms, this meant that the social-democratic parties were non-revolutionary, and were therefore un-Marxist, seeing that Marx had declared that the overthrow of the capitalist system could only be achieved by revolution. By rejecting revolution, these parties therefore became *ipso facto* "allies of the bourgeoisie", as to this day communist propaganda declares them to be.

According to this formulation, the *differentia* between the two parties is one of means rather than of ends, as it is assumed that they have the same objective—that is, that both wish to abolish private enterprise, set up a planned economy based on nationalized industries, and establish a classless society; and the indictment against the Social Democrats is that they reject what the Communists hold to be the only way in which this objective can be attained: which is by revolution, and not by reforms carried out gradually and in accordance with parliamentary procedure.

But however true this distinction may once have been, it has little meaning today. The whole purpose of present-day Communist techniques is to enable a party to seize power without a revolution at all, as it did in Czechoslovakia in February 1948. Again, the Communist Parties of Western Europe are fully aware that their best chance of securing it is to obtain parliamentary majorities, and both in France and Italy they have made strenuous efforts to get back into the governments from which they were excluded in 1947, and have not been

[1] *The Communist International. Documents 1919-23* (ed. Jane Degras), I, p. 239.

permitted to re-enter. Communist Parties are indeed opposed in principle to parliamentary government, and if they came into power they would abolish it, or merely preserve it as a façade. But this is logical enough seeing that parliamentary government rests on the assumption that in any society there will be sections with their own particular interests, and that these interests are best represented by political parties, each of which has the right to obtain a majority if it can. As the society which the Communists seek to establish is one from which all sections whose views differ from their own will have been eliminated, it is not easy to see how parliamentary government can continue to have a place in it; and indeed the British Socialist Party might well find it redundant if it ever succeeded in carrying out its full policy and reducing all members of the community to the condition which Professor L. H. Robbins has described as "propertyless uniformity".

The charge of gradualism brought against the Social Democrats is equally beside the point, seeing that the question is essentially one of degree. The Communists have never supposed that they could introduce their brand of Socialism overnight, and have thus found themselves obliged to practise gradualism even in the satellite countries where they have had a relatively free hand. The fact that Communist Parties have been enjoined by the Twentieth Congress to enter into coalitions with other left-wing groups in order to promote their policies by parliamentary means itself commits them to gradualism, as it does also to reformism, the practice of which is held to divide true Marxists from social democratic renegades.

But the Social Democrats have not only been accused by the Communists of being non-revolutionary in the sense of refusing to adopt the measures necessary to carry out a programme assumed to be common to both parties, which was Lenin's in-

dictment against Kautsky; they have also, and more frequently, been charged with abandoning the revolutionary tradition by compromising with their principles in such a manner
as to show that they do not intend to carry out their programme
at all. Here the Communists are on firmer ground. Traditionally,
Socialism has stood for the abolition of private enterprise, on
which the capitalist system is based, and the transference of the
means of production to the community, as it was regarded as
axiomatic that the result of this would be to liberate the pent-
up energies of the workers, who would redouble their exer-
tions to increase production in the industries they now owned.
Experience, at least in England, has failed, however, to con-
firm that this is so, and has led the right-wing Socialists to
conclude that, undesirable as private enterprise may be in
principle, it would be imprudent to abolish it, since it alone
provides the wherewithal to finance the Welfare State and discharge the liabilities incurred by the nationalized industries.
Indeed, nationalization has become so discredited that the discovery has recently been made that Socialism is not "about it"
at all, but "about equality"—a slogan better calculated to
appeal to the class which supports the Party at elections, and one
which, if applied, does not raise, at least immediately, awkward
questions as to increased production. Should the above become
the official doctrine, it would certainly provide a *differentia* between Socialism and Communism. For not only do the Communists insist upon nationalization, but they reject "equalitarianism" (*q.v.*), for which there is no authority in classical
Marxism, seeing that Engels specifically restricted its meaning
to freedom from "exploitation". It is true that in the years immediately following the seizure of power by the Bolsheviks,
the remuneration of party members was limited to "workers'
wages". But this practice had been abandoned long before
Stalin's famous "uravnilovka" speech of 1931, in which he

condemned the levelling down of the wages of factory and farm workers as a "petty bourgeois deviation". Since then, the Soviet leaders have resolutely opposed equalitarianism as failing to provide the necessary incentive for building up the industrial strength of the country, on which the future of Communism as a world movement depends.

Thus Social Democracy is not altogether easy to define. None the less, Social Democratism has acquired a certain currency of recent years as a term of abuse which the leadership of a Communist Party can apply to any of its members who sponsor policies which are allegedly social democratic. At the Plenum of the Central Committee of the East German Communist Party (the S.E.D.) of August 1952 Wilhelm Zaisser and Rudolf Herrnstadt were accused of it and were expelled from the Central Committee on account of the attitude they were said to have adopted at the time of the Berlin rising of the previous June, the specific charges against them being that they had advocated "capitulationism", and had exalted the spontaneous role of the masses at the expense of the Party, thus falling into the characteristic social democratic error of "tailism" (q.v.).

Again, in March 1954, the same charge was brought against Lecœur, who was accused of seeking to convert the Party into an amorphous mass, without effective organization in the field of labour, in which only a few communist groups were active—a conception which was declared to be a social democratic one, and calculated in the long run to bring about the liquidation of the party.

An article by the Czech Communist, Antonin Novotny, published in the *Cominform Journal* of December 11th 1953 summarizes the matter. It declares that Social Democratism "seeks to isolate the working-class from other sections of the working people, particularly from the peasants and intelligentsia"; that it displays itself in a tendency towards equalitarianism, that is, that all workers should share alike "irrespective of . . . the work performed, thereby flagrantly contradicting the principles of Socialism"; that it weakens "the general principle of party building, that of democratic centralism"; and that in the sphere of ideology it "manifests itself in distorting and vulgarizing Marxist-Leninist theory". From this the writer concludes that it is a dangerous form of bourgeois ideology, and should be combated as such.

46

SOCIALIST REALISM

THE introduction of the first Five-Year Plan was followed by a campaign to tighten up ideology, in the course of which literature, music and the arts duly received attention. In 1930 a conference held at Kharkov adopted Stalin's dictum that proletarian art must be "national in form and socialist in content", and passed a resolution that it should be placed in future under "the careful yet firm guidance of the Communist Party". The Decree of the Central Committee of April 23rd 1932 "On the Reorganization of Art and Literary Organizations" was a landmark in the development of totalitarian control in this field. It replaced the loosely-knit Union of Proletarian Writers by a single Union of Soviet Writers, and foreshadowed a similar centralized direction of other forms of art. The term "socialist realism" was not employed in the decree, but was coined almost immediately after as the slogan of the now unified literary movement. It appeared for the first time in an editorial in the *Literary Gazette* of May 29th 1932, and was later ascribed personally to Stalin.[1]

[1] For this see Andrey Olkhovsky, *Music under the Soviets* (New York, 1955), pp. 278–9. Soviet textbooks declare that the expression was first used in this year by Stalin in the course of a conversation with a group of writers. No further particulars are given. See also A. A. Adamovich, "Socialist

The *Large Soviet Encyclopædia* defines socialist realism as "A means of reflecting life in art peculiar to socialist society. It demands the true portrayal of reality in its revolutionary development. The problem of literature is the truthful and profound delineation of a new people, creators of socialist society, and of their fight for Communism . . .". In its directive to the Second All-Union Congress of Writers of 1954, the Central Committee pointed out that "to be capable of fulfilling the task of socialist realism calls for a thorough knowledge of the actual life of the people, of their feelings and ideas, and for a penetrating sensitivity to their experience . . ."; and an unsigned article in *Questions of Philosophy* (No. 4, 1955) described this directive as an "historical document of tremendous importance for the futher elucidation of the problems of socialist realism", though in fact it only repeated in somewhat more moderate terms the views set out in the various resolutions of the years 1946–48, when a large-scale drive for ideological orthodoxy was being conducted under Zhdanov's leadership.

The directive was currently stated to have been inspired by the "great solicitude" of the Central Committee for increasing the "spiritual wealth of the Soviet people". As the above article declared:

"In the period of the completion of the building of Socialism and the gradual transition to Communism in our country, when the Party is inspiring the whole nation for the solution of great historical problems, a tremendous part is played by the correct impressions of millions of people about the beauties of a labouring, creative life, about the socialist and communist ideal as the most majestic and brilliant aim of

Realism and its current aspects" in the *Report on the Soviet Union in 1956*, published by the Institute for the Study of the U.S.S.R. in Munich, and containing the proceedings of a conference held at the Carnegie International Center, New York, on April 28th–29th 1956, p. 100.

humanity; both our art and our aesthetic science are called upon constantly to instil this idea in the minds of Soviet people. That is why the Communist Party steadfastly directs the activities of Soviet writers and artists to the creation of deeply true, highly ideological and artistically perfect works of art, capable of educating the people in a communist spirit".

This is still the official doctrine. Thus, for example, A. Gerasimov, the President of the U.S.S.R. Academy of Arts, and one of the most uncompromising exponents of socialist realism, writing in *Social Culture* of March 27th 1956, said that some artists and critics had recently suggested that "the heritage of impressionism" could be made to serve the cause of socialist realism. But Gerasimov could not agree, though he admitted that impressionism had certain achievements to its credit, as it had, for example, "refreshed the artist's palette".

"For what", he asked, "have the impressionists reflected in their art? Lenin in one of his articles described 'intellectual impressionists' as men who 'spinelessly yield to the mood of the minute'. Naturally, impressionism, based on a momentary impression of nature, on its fleeting perception, on the fixation of chance phenomena, is opposed to the art of socialist realism which demands that the artist knows how to reveal the content of life . . . and that art takes part in the struggle for Communism. A fleeting perception of the facts of reality is clearly insufficient; what is needed is a progressive outlook that will help the artist to grasp and generalize correctly and deeply the phenomena of contemporary reality and create characters of broad social significance".

What all this means is that the Soviet leaders regard the arts solely as vehicles of propaganda, and that, as they do not care to admit this in so many words, the doctrine of socialist realism has been excogitated to provide a theoretical justification. At the same time, they are well aware that its application to literature has led to the production of innumerable dreary potboilers, a phenomenon which has had its counter-part in other fields of art. But this raises the problem of what are to be the canons of aesthetic judgement. The author of the article in *Questions of Philosophy* frankly deplores "the theoretical feebleness of our aesthetics", which he admits "has its categories like every other science". He complains, however, that there is a "lack of interest" in the subject, and holds, characteristically enough, that a "serious obstacle" to its fruitful development is "the organizational muddle that exists even to the present day in the work of training and employing cadres of workers in aesthetics", from which it would appear that the subject is being neglected in the higher centres of Marxist–Leninist learning. Indeed, the article complains, there exists no adequate literature upon the subject. The theories of such men as Belinsky and Chernyshevsky have not been explored, and, what is worse, "for many years not a word has appeared in print about the aesthetic views of Marx, Engels, Lenin and Stalin".

In fact, Marxist–Leninist principles make it impossible to formulate any theory of aesthetics at all. Every work of art is an act of self-expression. But in the Soviet Union self-expression is highly suspect, seeing that there is held to exist an objective reality which is independent of the artist, so that it is his duty to conform to it in whatever may be his medium. For as an article in *Bolshevik* of May 15th 1948 puts it,

"Socialist realism . . . establishes as the basis of artistic creation not the subjective, arbitrary ideas of the writer, but his detection of objective reality. The degree of artistry in the works of Soviet realist writers is determined primarily by the extent to which they accurately reproduce the course of the life process . . . ."

But what this objective reality may be, only the Party knows. Thus the *Large Soviet Encyclopædia* insists that if the artist is to reach the ideal which socialist realism imposes, he must be completely imbued with "party-mindedness" (*q.v.*), which is obviously very desirable, since the more he lives and moves and has his being in the Party, the more will his work be likely to represent what it wants. If the competent authorities are satisfied with it, the fact that it is a reflection, as it must needs be, of the individuality of its author will not arouse criticism, as he will have shown himself able to tune in to objective reality; whereas if they are not satisfied, he will be told that he has departed from "the scientific-objective, true party attitude", that he has allowed himself to be governed by his own tastes and feelings, and that he is therefore guilty of aesthetic objectivism which is scarcely removed, if indeed it is at all, from idealism.

47

SPONTANEITY

THE *Short History of the C.P.S.U.* (*b*) defines spontaneity as the doctrine that Socialists "should not try to impart a socialist consciousness to the working-class, but should wait until the spontaneous movement of the working-class arrives by itself at a socialist consciousness".

In Marx's system, the development of society, or of production—which amounts to the same thing—takes place through a dialectical process governed by objective laws which operate independently of the will of men. He assumed, however, that *pari passu* with this process, and as a function of it, there would develop in the proletariat, as a spontaneous and elemental force, that quality of class-consciousness which would enable the workers, in the fulness of time, to seize power; and he laid great stress, especially in his later writings, upon the necessity of developing this quality by education and organization. This view was shared by all the western socialist parties, and was enshrined in the slogan of the First International that "The emancipation of the workers can only be achieved by the workers themselves".

Lenin, however, challenged it by attacking in his *What is to be Done?* (1902) what he described as "subservience to spontaneity", his target being the "Economist" group in the Russian Social Democratic Labour Party which contended that proletarian action should be restricted to the economic field—that is, to trade unionism—and that revolutionary class-consciousness would spontaneously develop through such activity. (See "economism".) To this view he opposed the following propositions: (1) that "without a revolutionary theory there can be no revolutionary movement", (2) that the workers are incapable of producing such a theory since "the history of all countries shows that the working-class exclusively, by its own efforts, is able to develop only trade union consciousness", which is "ideological enslavement to the bourgeoisie", (3) that it must therefore be provided for them by the intelligentsia—the class from which his own Bolshevik Party was later to be recruited, and (4) that in consequence "all worship of the spontaneity of the labour movement, all belittling of the role of 'the conscious element', of the role of the party of Social Democracy . . . strengthens the influence of bourgeois ideology among the workers".[1]

On the question of the limitation of proletarian action to trade unionism Lenin gained his point, and the Economists were

[1] For an interesting discussion of Lenin's views on spontaneity see L. M. Haimson, *The Russian Marxists and the Origins of Bolshevism* (Harvard, 1956).

defeated at the Second Congress of 1903. But this by no means disposed of the matter, since, according to Lenin's interpretation, spontaneity was the assertion that the proletariat could makes its own revolution which was equivalent to a denial of the primary role of the party in bringing it about. For Lenin held that, if left to itself, the proletariat would never make a revolution at all, since it would inevitably compromise with the bourgeoisie in order to obtain, within the framework of the capitalist system, such concessions as would improve its working conditions, which was what the socialist parties of the West were doing in spite of the revolutionary programmes to which many of them were committed.

From this point of view there was much to be said for Lenin's position. Yet his rejection of spontaneity in fact raised a much larger issue as it implied a rejection of the determinist side of Marx's teaching. For revolutions no longer take place in obedience to objective laws, but because they have been willed by a group of professional revolutionaries specially trained in the art of organizing them. This, however, is a problem which calls for separate treatment, and is discussed under voluntarism below.

48

SUBJECTIVISM

ACCORDING to the *Oxford English Dictionary*, the subjective is that which "belongs, or is due to the sentient object as opposed to real and external things"; and thus, in the sphere of art, it is the expression of the artist's idiosyncrasy rather than of external reality. From our discussion of bourgeois objectivism and party-mindedness it will be apparent that such an attitude is inconsistent with the Marxist–Leninist doctrine, which assumes the existence of an objective reality, to which it is the duty both of the Party and its individual members to conform. Thus Lenin speaks of the danger of a party substituting "feelings" for "objective analysis", and in connection with the Brest-Litovsk treaty recontrasted those who were "revolutionaries out of sentiment" with "real revolutionaries".[1] It is, however, against individuals rather than against the Party that the charge of subjectivism is commonly levelled. The Party demands complete subjection to its will. But it is emphasized that this must not take the form of "blind obedience". Party members are enjoined to think for themselves, but at the same time to think as do the leaders, who are alone capable of perceiving the correct course of action. Thus subjectivism comes to mean any personal views or judgements which conflict with those of the leaders, and are therefore held to be injurious to the interests of the Party.

The term is also applied censoriously to any opinion which can be construed as a manifestation of subjective idealism, and can thus be twisted into a denial of the objective nature of reality and of the objective laws which govern it. Thus after the publication of Stalin's *Economic Problems of Socialism in the U.S.S.R.* (1952), with its insistence upon the objective laws of political economy, those economists who were held to have gone too far in their glorification of the Soviet State found themselves accused of it, though the main charge directed against them was one of "voluntarism" (*q.v.*).

49

TAILISM

ACCORDING to the *Political Dictionary*, "Tailism (*kvostism*) in the class struggle means a rejection of active revolutionary action, a denial of the leading role of the revolutionary party of

---

[1] Leites, *op. cit.*, p. 190.

the working-class". The term was coined by Lenin in his *What is to be Done?* (1902), where it is associated with "economism" and "spontaneity" (*q.q.v.*), the former being the view that trade union action is "the most widely applicable method of drawing the masses into the political struggle", while the latter contains by implication a denial of the primary role of the Party in the revolution. He was to return to this in his *One Step Forward, Two Steps Back* and his *Two Tactics*. The particular issues need not concern us. But what he is saying in both cases is that, in deference to public opinion, his opponents are adopting the line of least resistance by taking the easy path instead of the hard one. Tailism is thus the refusal of the Party to recognize that its duty is to lead the masses and not to follow their wishes, since, according to Lenin, these will be limited to the satisfaction of "concrete demands", and will always stop short of revolution. Thus while the Party is required to maintain the closest contact with the masses, it is not their mandatory, but rather the interpreter of what they would desire were they sufficiently mature to discern their real interests. There is an obvious connection between this and his conception of the "narrow" party consisting of an *élite*, whose more highly developed class-consciousness enables it to see further than those among whom it works, and thus justifies its claim to leadership. But this *élitism* is anti-democratic, and Lenin's insistence upon it reveals his profound distrust of the people, who do not "make the revolution", but are the raw material with which it is made.

50

VOLUNTARISM

VOLUNTARISM is the attribution of primary and decisive importance to the human will as the determinant of social change rather than to objective scientific laws. Marxist–Leninist theory has never found it easy to arrive at a balance between the two. What is it, for example, that brings a revolution about? Does it occur because some person or body of persons has willed it, or is it the outcome of a process which is working itself out in history through what Marx declared to be "inexorable laws"? It is the problem of the role of consciousness or will on the one hand and that of the material world of being on the other. Marx had sought to bring the two into a dynamic equilibrium, and as Vernon V. Aspaturian has pointed out, this was one of the most attractive features of his philosophy, as "it supported social purpose with scientific analysis, thus satisfying the two basic yearnings of the nineteenth century".[1]

None the less, in all Marx's writings and throughout his lifetime the determinist element in his system was everywhere emphasized in order to stress its scientific character, and it was with his Russian followers that there began the shift to voluntarism, which was in closer accord with the native revolutionary traditions as exemplified by Pestel, Tkachev and Bakunin and by the Populist movement. As Aspaturian says, a theoretical justification for it was supplied by Plekhanov, through whom Lenin received his initiation into Marxism, as Plekhanov attempted to meet the charge of "fatal determinism" levelled against the Marxist doctrine by its critics by stressing its activist side, and was the bridge between the later views of Engels and those which Lenin was to express.

In his *What is to be Done?* (1902) Lenin declared war on "spontaneity" (*q.v.*); that is, the view that the proletariat can itself make a revolution. He did not, indeed, dispute the existence of objective laws, as this would have been to repudiate the Marxist dialectic of history which he was genuinely concerned

[1] *The Contemporary Doctrine of the Soviet State and its Philosophical Foundations* (American Political Science Review, December 1954, pp. 1033–4).

to uphold. But he wanted to bring about a revolution, and believed that this would only be possible if the Party consisted of a relatively small number of self-dedicated professional revolutionaries. Such a conception of its nature may not indeed have been that of Marx. But Lenin might well have replied that there was no reason why it should be. For the form which the Party took depended on circumstances. If there was no revolutionary situation, a "mass party" which included sympathizers was clearly desirable, as this would attract the maximum degree of support, but once such a situation existed a "narrow party" was needed if it was to be exploited, as Marx would presumably have held that it should be.

Lenin was reasoning as a practical revolutionary, concerned to create the instrument appropriate to his purpose. Yet his thesis contained serious implications. According to Marx, the proletariat is brought into existence by the capitalist system, of which it is destined to be the "grave-digger", and thus its revolutionary role is part of an inexorable process. The two stand and fall together. Yet if what Lenin said was correct, as indeed it was, seeing that, as Max Eastman has pointed out, Marx wrongly attributes to the proletariat attitudes and judgements that belong only to little groups of revolutionaries,[1] it followed that, given sufficiently disturbed conditions, a body of trained agitators could at any time bring about a revolution without regard to those objective economic conditions upon which Marx, at least in theory, had set such store. And this has proved to be the case, as all communist revolutions have in fact been carried out by a hard core of professionals, and have been proletarian only in so far that the moment chosen has naturally been one when that class, and other sections of labour also, has had some special ground for discontent.

Thus Lenin gave Marx's teaching a voluntarist turn. The

[1] *Stalin's Russia and the Crisis of Socialism* (1940), p. 217.

primary reason why a revolution occurs is that the Party has decided that it should. Theoretically, it is true that the Party does not come to this decision until the "objective conditions" for the revolution have been created, but its success will naturally be taken as a proof that this was so. For the Bolsheviks, therefore, these conditions were a secondary factor, whereas the Mensheviks regarded them as all-important, and held that no proletarian revolution should be attempted until they could be shown to exist.

Stalin carried this voluntarist tendency still further. For some years after the Second World War, the achievements of the Soviet State had been extolled in terms so extravagant as to encourage the illusion that nothing was beyond its powers. But on the eve of the Nineteenth Congress of 1952 Stalin published his *Economic Problems of Socialism in the U.S.S.R.*, in which he dwelt with all possible emphasis upon the existence of objective economic laws by which even Soviet planners were bound; and one motive for thus drawing attention to this neglected aspect of the Marxist–Leninist creed may well have been to warn the public not to expect too much from the long-awaited congress. This was followed up by an article by Suslov in *Pravda* of December 24th attacking N. Vosnesensky, the author of a much-publicized book, *The War Economy of the U.S.S.R. in the Period of the Great Patriotic War*, and a former member of the Politbureau, who had been dismissed from his posts as head of the State Planning Commission (Gosplan) and deputy chairman of the Council of Ministers on March 15th 1949. This work was represented in a *Kommunist* leader of February 1953 as "a medley of subjectivist, idealist and voluntarist views", and Vosnesensky was accused of maintaining that "the development of socialist economy is determined by the will of the State, of its planning organs, that the State is the 'source of movement and development of the socialist economy', and that the planned direction by the State is a law of its development". The same criticism was made of a number of Soviet economists, who were accused of voluntarism for their neglect of "the Marxist formula of the objectivity of the laws of Socialism", an attitude which the above article described as "alien and hostile to the Marxist world outlook, the Soviet socialist system, and the cause of the construction of Socialism", though it was one that Stalin had done more than any man to encourage until he saw that the persistent "glorification of the achievements of the Soviet State" might have consequences embarrassing to the Party.

None the less, the present Communist outlook is very largely one of voluntarism. Revolutions are imposed "from above", though it is of course asserted that they are governed by economic laws. Marx, however, believed firmly in the dialectic of society, and this is still an article of faith, as it provides the movement with a pseudo-scientific philosophy, so that in all centres of communist learning its intricacies are expounded and its discrepancies explained away. Yet here, as elsewhere, the theoreticians have to walk warily. If they attribute too much importance to the will as expressed by that of the State or Party, they may be told that they are ignoring these objective laws of society which Marxist–Leninism regards as possessing the same status as the laws of the natural sciences; while if they dwell unduly upon these laws, they are likely to be told that they are underestimating the importance of the human element by refusing to recognize the creative role of the proletariat and of its revolutionary Party.

INDEX

WITHDRAWN